ENVIRONMENTAL IMPACT ASSESSMENT IN THE U

Background, Basics, Context and Procedure

Alan Bond

CP

Chandos Publishing (Oxford) Limited

ISBN 1 902375 42 4

Chandos Publishing (Oxford) Limited
Chandos House
5 & 6 Steadys Lane
Stanton Harcourt
Oxford OX8 1RL
England

Tel: 01865 882727 Fax: 01865 884448
Email: sales@chandospublishing.com
www.chandospublishing.com

Printed in England

ENVIRONMENTAL IMPACT ASSESSMENT IN THE UK

THE CHANDOS SERIES ON THE ENVIRONMENT

Contents

Appendices

ACKNOWLEDGEMENTS

The work that has gone into this book acknowledges the help and experience of others. In particular, much of the material has been developed from experience gained from Prof. Peter Wathern of the EIA Unit in Aberystwyth. Additionally, some materials have been developed from training courses put together by Sally Russell and/or Mandy King during their time in the EIA Unit.

Most of all, thanks are extended to my family, Gina, Angharad, Harry and Jack who have lost the time which was dedicated to the book instead of them.

PREFACE

The purpose of this book is to explain, in what it is hoped are simple but not patronising terms, what Environmental Impact Assessment (EIA) is all about in the United Kingdom. The specific aim of the book is to explain the new EIA procedure in the UK implemented as a result of the 1997 amendments to the European Union's Environmental Assessment Directive 1985. In doing this, the book makes clear the implications of the UK procedures to help readers from a wide range of backgrounds, and assumes no prior knowledge of EIA.

In order to cater for such a diverse audience, the book starts at the beginning, explaining EIA from first principles, what is involved in carrying out the process of EIA, the techniques available to help and the amount of work which is entailed. However, the book is not intended as a guide to carrying out EIA – other texts perform this function admirably.

Having explained what EIA means, the book also provides the background to its development as a legal process in the United Kingdom in 1988. This necessarily involves a consideration of the evolution of the National Environmental Policy Act 1969 in the United States of America (the world's first EIA legislation).

Consideration is also given to the entry of the UK into the European Union (EU) as this has continuing implications for the development of environmental legislation within the UK. The obligations imposed on member states like the United Kingdom by various types of EU legislation is explained, and specific reference is made to the influence Europe has had over the development of UK EIA regulations. Readers who are already familiar with this background can simply skip these chapters and move on to the consideration of the updated regulations. In some detail, the obligations of both the original 1985 Directive (85/337/EEC) and the amended Environmental Assessment Directive (97/11/EC) are considered.

To place EIA into its correct context within the UK, some consideration is also given to the planning system in England and Wales because, without this context, a new reader may not understand where EIA fits into the wider picture and how it can actually have an influence on decisions.

The regulations drafted in the UK to fulfil both the current and the previous obligations imposed by directives are considered, detailing the reasons behind the appearance of some regulations. Clear reference is made to the requirements imposed on planning authorities and developers alike, and their likely implications.

As well as the description provided of the UK procedure, a bibliography is provided which aims to list key reading material. The approach taken here is not encyclopaedic; rather the list of further reading material is brief but covers books, web pages, journals and UK government guidance on EIA in order to help readers easily delve more deeply into the subject area if they so wish.

LIST OF FIGURES

LIST OF TABLES

THE AUTHOR

Alan Bond achieved an honours degree in Environmental Science from the University of Lancaster in 1985 where he went on to spend three years researching for a PhD, studying 'the simulation of lava flows with small-scale models'. This essentially involved pouring mud down various slopes at various speeds and watching what happened. Such a background inevitably led to a career in research and development for Mars Confectionery in 1988, after having illustrated the similarities between the flow of lava and the flow of chocolate.

Three years later Alan decided it was time to concentrate on his environmental ideals and get back to the subject area where he had originally started. This involved enrolling on an Envionmental Impact Assessment MSc programme, followed by various research contracts at the University of Wales Aberystwyth before being appointed lecturer in 1994.

The author still lectures in Environmental Impact Assessment at the University of Wales in Aberystwyth, and is resident in Aberystwyth with his partner and 2.5 children. He may be contaced through the publishers.

CHAPTER 1

What is EIA?

This chapter covers some introductory concepts of EIA. Briefly, it defines what is meant by EIA and then considers the essential elements of the EIA process, explaining what happens at each stage. This brief coverage distinguishes between the terms process (which refers to a generic description of what EIA is about) and procedure (which refers to the legal requirements which indicate which of the stages must take place as part of EIA in a particular country). Finally, as so much of EIA is about making decisions on the significance and/or magnitude of impacts, a separate section is devoted to explaining the meaning of these terms.

1.1   Definitions

Environmental Impact Assessment is normally abbreviated to the acronym EIA, although the same process can go under other titles as well. In fact the term 'impact' is often dropped (particularly in the United Kingdom) and the title Environmental Assessment used, the argument being that the term impact itself suggests negative outcomes. Others use just the term Impact Assessment (IA), dropping the term environment, which would suggest a narrow definition possibly ignoring social and economic consequences. This book will stick to the term Environmental Impact Assessment and define its scope accordingly. Unfortunately, the different names attributed to EIA are not just a question of semantics. EIA is normally a legal process and, as a result, the precise nature of what is to be assessed – and for what – is often clearly set out. The problem is that, while we can generalise about what EIA is, the legal process is different in many countries around the world; this inevitably leads to confusion and is the reason why we need to consider a number of definitions of EIA here.

However, there is no agreed definition of what EIA is or entails. Box 1 details some of the more commonly known definitions which help to give a flavour of what it is all about.

Box 1 EIA definitions

'EIA can be described as a process for identifying the likely consequences for the biogeophysical environment and for man's health and welfare of implementing particular activities and for conveying this information, at a stage when it can materially affect their decision, to those responsible for sanctioning the proposals.'

(Wathern, 1988, p. 6)

'Environmental impact assessment ... is best treated as a generic term for a process that seeks to blend administration, planning, analysis and public involvement in assessment prior to the taking of a decision.'

(Barrow, 1997, p. 1)

' "Environmental Impact Assessment" (EIA) can be defined as the systematic identification and evaluation of the potential impacts (effects) of proposed projects, plans, programs, or legislative actions relative to the physical-chemical, biological, cultural, and socio-economic components of the total environment.'

(Canter, 1996, p. 2).

'In essence, EIA is a *process*, a systematic process that examines the environmental consequences of development actions, in advance. The emphasis, compared with many other mechanisms for environmental protection, is on prevention.'

(Glasson et al., 1994, p. 3)

'*Environmental impact assessment (EIA)* The official appraisal of the likely effects of a proposed policy, program, or project on the environment; alternatives to the proposal; and measures to be adopted to protect the environment.'

(Gilpin, 1995, pp. 4–5)

The list of definitions could go on. At this stage, however, bearing in mind the relevance of this book to the UK case, it is useful to give just one more definition – that of the UK Department of the Environment in their guidance to accompany UK legislation on EIA (see Box 2). Note that this definition is directly relevant to just one legal procedure as opposed to being a general definition of the process itself.

Box 2 UK Department of the Environment definition of EIA

'The term "environmental assessment" describes a technique and a process by which information about the environmental effects of a project is collected, both by the developer and from other sources, and taken into account by the planning authority in forming their judgement on whether the development should go ahead.'

(Department of the Environment, 1989, p. 3)

At this stage, we will not cloud the issue further by attempting to offer a definition which aims to draw together those already listed. The reason that it is so difficult to find an agreed definition for EIA is that it means many things to many people. Those involved in EIA range from decision-makers through to developers through to the public; the roles and needs of these different groups are very different, both within and between countries. It is these different perspectives that make EIA such an interesting subject area – and also quite an aggravating one!

The definition in Box 2 refers to the assessment of the impacts of *projects*. The reader should be aware that this is a limited definition and that it is possible (preferable would be a better word) to assess the impacts of *policies*, *programmes* and *plans*. Such assessments are normally described as Strategic Environmental Assessments (SEA) and are already common in the UK (local authorities, for example, are required to carry out strategic appraisals of their development plans). SEAs have an important role to play in controlling, in particular, cumulative impacts. If we consider that the implications for the environment of one project might not be so serious, then it is likely to be approved. But what if ten such developments are all approved, each without serious impacts? It may be the case that, together, the impacts are a real problem – hence the need for SEA. SEAs are not the focus of this book but interested readers can refer to Therivel et al. (1992) or Therivel and Partidário (1996) for a greater insight.

In order to set the scene for the rest of the book, it is also important to understand the term *impact* itself. Figure 1.1 represents what is meant by the term impact. Basically, an impact occurs where any parameter changes from the value it would have had without the project. This makes it sound rather scientific, but it is also the case that where a view of scenery changes, then that is an impact and it can be positive (for example, a view can improve, pollution can be reduced) as well as negative.

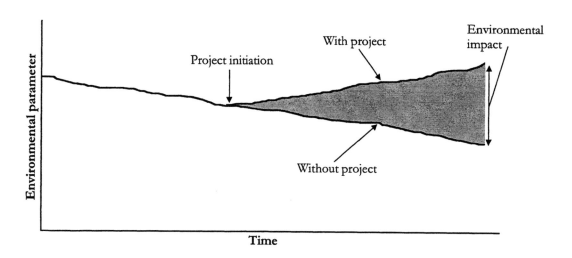

Figure 1.1 Diagrammatic representation of an environmental impact.

It is too simplistic to consider that impacts are directly related to one action (like a specific development). In reality, many developments take place which can all have an effect on the environment – whether it be affecting the view, the quality of a river, etc. It is important that the cumulative impacts due to a combination of factors are recognised because the overall effect on the environment can be far more dramatic – as illustrated in Figure 1.2.

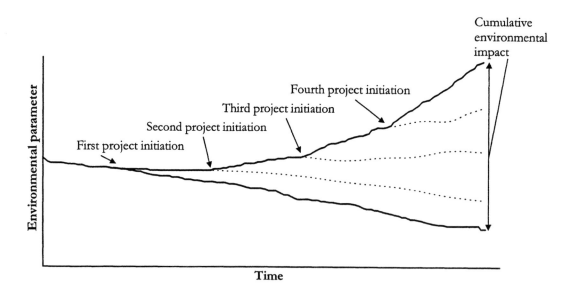

Figure 1.2 Diagrammatic representation of a cumulative environmental impact.

A number of types of cumulative impact exist as defined in Box 3.

Box 3 Types of cumulative impact

- *Additive impacts* may occur with projects which individually are too small to require an EIA (under existing legislation). In particular, this applies to many agricultural projects, and in countries which have legally defined thresholds this can pose a significant problem because developers have an incentive to favour developments of a size just below that of the threshold.

- *Synergistic impacts* are caused when the total impact of several projects is greater than the sum of their individual impacts. These sorts of impacts are particularly evident in relation to air pollution where a combination of certain pollutants from different developments can lead to human health problems.

- *Threshold/saturation impacts* are caused because the environment only has a limited capacity to recover from pollution. Recovery will occur up to a certain level, beyond which permanent damage may occur. An example would be a stream which is subject to the discharge of several chemicals; another factory discharging into the stream could push it past its capability for self-purification and kill off life within it.

- *Induced and indirect impacts* are created by certain developments encouraging the proliferation of other developments. The most obvious example is roads, where the improved access favours other types of development; motorways in particular cause this effect and are almost guaranteed to lead at least to the development of service stations.

- *Time-crowded or space-crowded impacts* occur in situations where the environment does not have time to recover between impacts. An example of this is forestry operations, with a rapid rotation period which does not allow recovery, thus causing a loss of soil productivity.

The description of types of cumulative impacts in Box 3 includes *indirect impacts* which are not only cumulative in nature. Impacts resulting directly from a single development can have indirect impacts. For example, a common indirect impact resulting from a new bypass road is the collapse of some small businesses which relied on a certain number of vehicles stopping to buy goods in the town or village which has been bypassed.

The European Commission of the EU commissioned the production of *Guidelines for the Assessment of Indirect and Cumulative Impacts as well as Impact Interactions* which was published in 1999 (Walker and Johnston, 1999). This is a useful document for people wishing to know more about impacts.

1.2   Process or procedure?

We can consider EIA as either a process or a procedure. The meaning of these two terms, however, is different and they will be defined here for the purposes of this book.

The EIA process may be considered a generic, possibly even ideal process for carrying out environmental impact assessment. An EIA procedure, on the other hand, is a specific set of legal instructions for carrying out the EIA. The position in the UK illustrates the difference: in the UK, there are specific regulations which set out exactly what must be done in order to fulfil environmental impact assessment obligations. However, the UK procedure does not include all of the stages of the EIA process.

Figure 1.3 is a simplistic diagram of the EIA process showing a linear progression of changes. In reality, the process is much more complicated and the diagram will be developed once the broad concepts have been introduced. The figure lists a series of stages which comprise the overall process and indicates the order in which these stages take place. Below we give a brief description of what is involved in each of the stages indicated in Figure 1.3 to facilitate understanding of what is meant by the term process. After this brief overview, each of the stages will be examined in more detail in section 1.3 to indicate what is actually involved.

1.2.1   Consideration of alternatives

At the concept stage of any development, a number of alternative ways of proceeding can be considered such as design or location alternatives. Suppose an electricity generating company needs to increase capacity. There are a number of ways in which extra energy can be produced: from oil, gas or coal as fuel for a power station or by means of hydro-power, solar power or even wind power. Which of these alternatives is chosen will depend on factors such as cost and current government policy, among others.

There is also the issue of where the generating capacity will be sited. The type of power station will restrict the possible sites, but then there are a large number of alternatives to choose from.

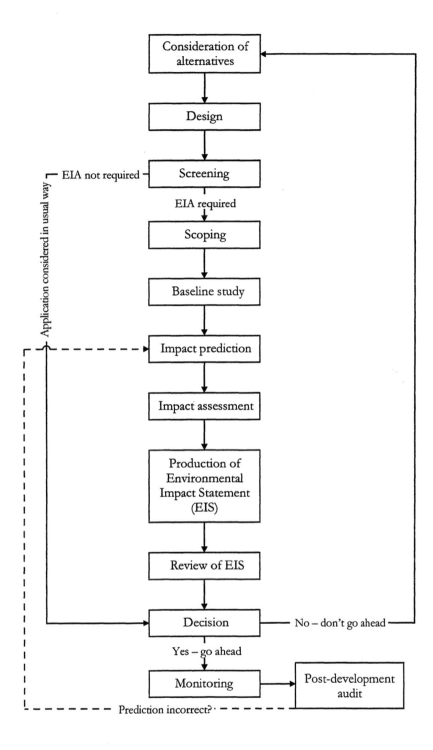

Figure 1.3 Simplified EIA process.

1.2.2   Design

Once the alternative choices have been considered, the actual design itself can take place. This involves specific choices regarding the siting of the various components of the development such as car parks, paths and buildings. The design choices can have significant implications for the impacts which result. For example, a development which will produce a lot of noise can be designed so that noisy machinery is restricted to the centre of the site, using other buildings to shield areas outside the boundaries of the site.

1.2.3   Screening

The EIA process begins at the very initiation of a project. By this, we mean the time when the project is first considered, not when construction begins. Once a developer has identified a need, assessed all the realistic alternatives of project design and sites and selected a preferred alternative, important questions must be asked: 'What might the effects of this development be on the environment, and are those effects important?' If a development is likely to have impacts on the environment, then it is imperative that a decision is made on whether a formal EIA will have to take place to take into account these impacts (positive and negative) – this is known as the screening decision. The EIA process is, it must be stressed, iterative. This is demonstrated at this early stage of screening where the requirement for a formal EIA and its associated cost implications can lead the developer to reassess the project design with a view to reducing the significant impacts to a level where an EIA is not legally required.

1.2.4   Scoping

Where it is decided that a formal EIA is required, the next stage is to define the issues which need to be addressed, i.e. those impacts which might have a significant effect on the environment. This is known as scoping and is essential for focusing the available resources on the relevant issues. An EIA carried out without a proper scoping exercise is in danger of wasting a lot of time and effort on investigations which aren't necessary or even relevant to the particular development in question. For example, consider again the example of an electricity-generating project: assuming generation from wind power, it is likely that we would focus on visual and noise impacts, among others. It is not the case that we would want to spend time and money on investigations into air pollution produced by the wind turbines or on possible thermal water pollution more typical of projects involving energy generated from fossil fuel.

1.2.5   Baseline study

Production of an EIS then involves a number of steps which are themselves iterative. The first of these is, for the scoped issues, to gather all the required baseline information. This is information on the current status of the environment likely to be affected by the development, and must take account of current trends so that the status of the environment in the future, in the absence of the development, can be predicted. This study is referred to as a baseline study.

1.2.6   Impact prediction

Once the baseline study information is available, the important task of impact prediction can begin. Impact prediction is forecasting the change in the environmental parameter in question because of the presence of the development. This step is crucial for an effective EIA as this is where the problem issues are investigated in a scientific way. Ideally, this stage should indicate the predicted magnitude of an impact, i.e. just how big it really will be. For our example of a windfarm development, a predicted impact would be the increase in noise levels experienced by residents close to the wind turbines.

1.2.7   Impact assessment

The necessary next phase then involves an analysis of the predicted impacts to determine both their importance and significance; this is known as impact assessment. The aim of impact assessment is to provide a conclusion which can ultimately be used by the decision-makers to support the determination of the project application. Just because an impact is large does not necessarily mean that it is significant as significance depends on many other factors. For the wind farm example we have been considering, the predicted increase in noise in a residence may be 10 dBA (unit of measurement for noise level) – assessing the impact tries to answer the question: what does this change in noise level mean to the residents of the property? Will they notice it? If they notice it, will they be disturbed by it? Will it stop them sleeping at night? Affirmative answers to each of these question in turn clearly increases the significance of the impact. However, the assessment has to look at the bigger picture – if just one residence is affected (but affected very badly), how does that balance against the net benefit gained by having the project?

1.2.8   *Producing the environmental impact statement*

The outcome of an EIA is usually a document known as an Environmental Impact Statement (EIS), which sets out the factual information relating to the development and all the information relating to screening, scoping, baseline study, impact prediction and assessment, and mitigation and monitoring measures. It is commonly a requirement for an EIS that a Non-Technical Summary (NTS) be included. This is simply a summary of the information contained within the EIS, presented in a non-technical format so that the lay person can easily understand it. This is very important, as EISs are public documents intended to inform the public of the nature and likely consequences of a development in time to comment on and/or participate in the project design.

1.2.9   *EIS review*

Once the EIA is complete, the EIS is submitted to the competent authority. This is the body with the authority to permit or refuse the development application. The competent authorities are often in a position of having very little time to make a decision and having a detailed and lengthy EIS to read through which may contain errors, omissions and developer bias. It is essential, therefore, that they review the document. Review can take a number of forms: it may be purely an unstructured process whereby the document is read and commented on by decision-makers; it can be more formalised whereby expert opinions are sought on points raised; it can be via a review method designed specifically for the purpose. Basically, the review process should enable the decision-maker to conclude whether the EIA has been adequate, whether the information is correct, whether it is unbiased, and whether further information is required.

The decision-makers are now in possession of the information they require about the possible effects of the development on the environment. They will use this information, in combination with all of the other details and representations they have received, to help them come to a decision.

1.2.10 Monitoring

Now is the appropriate time to implement monitoring measures. Monitoring is defined in Chapter 7 of Wathern (1988) as 'an activity undertaken to provide specific information on the characteristics and functioning of environmental and social variables in space and time'. Monitoring may also have been undertaken at the baseline study phase to determine the pre-development trends. Basically, monitoring should be undertaken to determine whether the impact predictions were accurate and ensure that no unexpected effects are occurring.

It is important to stress that the design of monitoring measures should have taken place at the same time as the development itself was designed. If this is not done, monitoring becomes an afterthought which may be badly planned, poorly resourced and, therefore, ineffective.

1.2.11 Post-development audit

Once the development is in place, a Post Development Audit (PDA) should be carried out to check whether the predictions made in the EIA were correct. This process should help improve the standard of predictions in the future with, as a consequence, better decisions being made on development applications because the decision-makers are in possession of better information.

So that is the EIA process, but what about an EIA procedure? By this is meant the legal procedure as set out in the legislation of a particular country. The difference should be fairly clear. Any particular country could choose which of the stages of the EIA process were useful to it and legislate accordingly. For example, there is no requirement in the UK to monitor impacts or to carry out post-development audits (and this is not unusual – these stages are rare in EIA procedures).

What has been missed out of the explanation so far is a consideration of mitigation. The whole point of EIA is that it is a systematic means of identifying impacts and reducing them or removing them altogether. In some cases this may not be possible and there may be some residual impacts. It is not the case that mitigation fits into the process as an individual stage – there are a number of occasions on which mitigation measures may be identified. Figure 1.4 amends Figure 1.3 and shows some possible linkages with mitigation.

1.2.12 Mitigation

Frequently, the assessment of impacts will reveal damaging effects upon the environment. These can be alleviated by mitigation measures. Mitigation involves taking measures to reduce or remove environmental impacts and it can be seen that the iterative nature of the EIA process is well demonstrated here. Successful design of mitigation measures may result in the removal of all significant impacts, hence a new screening exercise would remove the need to carry out a formal EIA.

From Figure 1.4 it becomes apparent that an EIA evolves as it goes along and there is no way of forecasting exactly what will happen at what stage in the proceedings. This representation of the process is also simplified in that it completely ignores the openness of the process. Good EIA requires that the public, particularly those likely to be affected by the proposals, is given an opportunity to feed into the process. There is no reason why this input can't happen at all of the stages of the process.

As well as public input, there is also a need for expert input from groups other than the developers, who clearly have a vested interest in the outcome. Thus, it is common for consultations to take place with organisations having specific environmental responsibilities under law – these organisations are known as statutory consultees in this context. Figure 1.5 amends Figure 1.4 and indicates where such participation might occur in the EIA process.

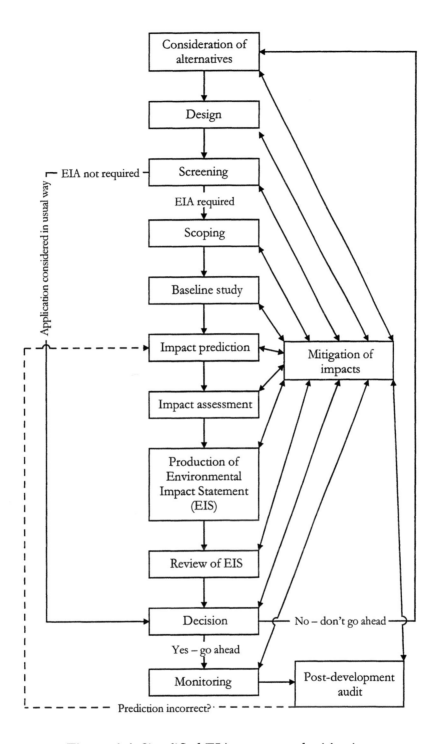

Figure 1.4 Simplified EIA process and mitigation.

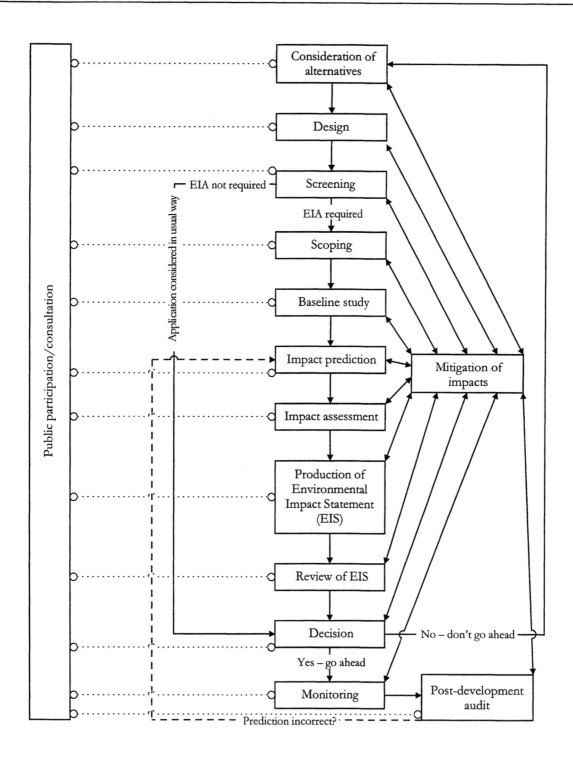

Figure 1.5 The EIA process.

1.2.13 Public participation

The public should be extensively involved in EIA and, if successful, public participation can help to ensure that the development meets approval and is not environmentally unacceptable. Successful public participation has been described as (O'Sullivan et al., 1999):

- efficiently obtaining information from the public;

- including all the stakeholders;

- increasing understanding and acceptance of the project;

- satisfying the public with regard to their degree of involvement.

While good public participation is universally considered to be a good thing, on a cautionary note it should be remembered that uncoordinated release of project information can lead to misinterpretation by the public and could facilitate scaremongering.

Including public participation in Figure 1.5 means that we now have a figure which represents what happens in the EIA process, although you should be aware that only the major linkages are drawn into this figure. The whole process is iterative and many feedback loops can develop. In a later chapter, a similar flow chart will be introduced to represent the specific EIA procedure in place in the United Kingdom – it will be interesting to compare that procedure with the process shown here.

Hopefully you now understand what is meant by the term 'EIA process', and which particular stages go to make up a complete EIA process. The preceding description was kept deliberately brief so as not to lose sight of the overall picture and so that you would appreciate where each stage fitted into the process as a whole. Having gained this understanding, it is now appropriate to move onto a fuller description of the various process stages.

1.3   The EIA process in detail

In order to consider in detail the stages in the EIA process outlined above, they have to be taken separately to make discussion easier. The temptation to assume that the order of the following headings dictates the order in which these stages are carried out in practice should be avoided for the reasons described above. This is especially true for public participation which should occur throughout the process but has been included first to encourage any practitioners reading this book to get their public participation programme in place early on.

1.3.1   *Public participation*

Public participation is a, if not the, key component of EIA. It has long been recognised that good public participation is essential if EIA is to be effective and, ultimately, to lead to development which is acceptable to all those with a vested interest.

In Europe and in many countries of the world, the public participation component of EIA is traditionally weak and does little to involve, in a constructive way, communities affected by developments. It is encouraging to know that this is now changing and that the amended European Union Directive on Environmental Assessment (97/11/EC), for example, did strengthen considerably the public information requirements. Even more refreshing is the fact that the European Commission is already privately acknowledging that the European Union's signing of the Århus Convention means that the amended EIA Directive will have to be amended again to improve public participation! So what is the Århus Convention?

Briefly, the full title of the Convention is 'Convention on Access to Information, Public Participation in Decision-Making and Access to Justice in Environmental Matters'. It is a document which was finalised at Århus in Denmark in June 1998 and is the responsibility of the United Nations Economic Commission for Europe. Articles 4, 5 and 6 of this Convention refer to 'access to environmental information', 'collection and dissemination of environmental information' and 'public participation in decisions on specific activities' respectively. As well as these specific articles, article 9 on 'access to justice' requires all signatories to have in place a free or cheap appeals procedure in cases where access to environmental information as specified in article 4 has been denied. This effectively means a cheap form of process akin to judicial review, although this will only be available to parties with sufficient standing.

To date, 39 countries as diverse as Armenia and the UK, Kazakhstan and Switzerland, have signed the Convention and will be bound by its terms upon ratification (United Nations Economic Commission for Europe, 1999). Those signatories which have EIS systems in place are thus likely to have to amend their EIA procedures. Outside those 39 countries, it seems almost inconceivable that such a dramatic increase in public participation within the EIA process will not follow in countries not also bound by the aims of the Århus Convention as resident populations will expect equivalent rights.

Public participation should adhere to certain rules, namely that participation should be:

- started early and occur throughout the process (with defined cycles of activity);

- interactive – a two-way process including feedback; and

- inclusive, transparent and honest.

(O'Sullivan and Bond, 1999)

While this seems simple enough, it is important to understand exactly what is meant by the term 'participation'. In 1969, Arnstein presented a ladder of participation which has been referred to ever since to help to explain this term and its relationship to other, related, forms of public involvement. The ladder indicates a number of steps of increasing involvement of the public, starting from no real involvement at the bottom and reaching citizen control at the top (a variation on Arnstein's original ladder is shown in Figure 1.6).

Petts (1999) lists techniques such as leaflets, advertising, local newspapers, television and radio, video, exhibitions, telephone helplines and newsletters as being on the participation level of information provision; interviews and surveys on the level of information collection and feedback (this is not one of the levels indicated in Figure 1.6 but falls between information provision and consultation); public meetings and small group meetings on the level of consultation; and community advisory groups and workshops as being on the level of participation.

To enhance the public participation process, then, a number of techniques can be identified which might be appropriate, depending on the nature of the development and the affected communities. These are:

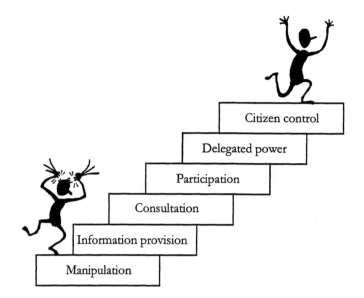

Figure 1.6 Some different levels of public participation.

(Adapted from Petts, 1999; Arnstein, 1969.)

- *Open houses* – a staffed display at convenient locations, which the public is invited to visit to discuss the proposals and to provide verbal and written comments.

- *Planning workshops* – meetings involving the developer, the community and non-governmental organisation (NGO) representatives at which views are discussed and strategies developed for resolving points of disagreement. These meetings have a neutral facilitator and should distribute minutes widely.

- *Community advisory committees* – groups of people formed to represent the community in their dealings with the developer.

- *Citizens' juries and consensus conferences* – a small representative panel of people is chosen to reflect the views of a community and develop their understanding of relevant issues by speaking to experts of their own choosing. The findings of the panel are publicised. Consensus conferences are less formal than citizens' juries, though both processes are costly.

- *Participative social impact assessment and management* – a process using a combination of advertisements in the local media and open houses, in which the public is encouraged to indicate views on specific questions relating to the assessment and management of the social impacts of a proposal.

A more in-depth consideration of public participation techniques and their level of participation can be found in Petts (1999).

The public need to be actively involved in the EIA process so that their concerns can be recognised early on and addressed. While early involvement is generally recognised as being beneficial, it is not always possible or recommended at the design stage of a project or where alternatives are being considered because of the alarm which may result. Indeed, in terms of confidentiality issues, some would argue that the involvement of the public prior to a planning application being made and an EIA having been finished is too soon (see Petts, 1999). However, it is becoming more accepted that public participation, done properly, will benefit the developer in terms of ensuring good design and project acceptability. Certainly in terms of coverage of appropriate issues in an EIA, public participation should be part of scoping.

Having embarked upon a development project which requires an EIA, a developer has a number of important factors to consider when communicating with the public:

- How many people can be involved in the participation exercise? The more the better as far as the community will be concerned, but cost and time constraints will be acting to keep numbers lower. It may also be impractical to involve everybody unless a manageable number of representatives are used.

- Can the communication method deal with specific issues? If the method used is that of posting leaflets, it will be general in nature, and will not be able to address any specific concerns which the public may have in the absence of any feedback.

- Can the method provide good two-way communication? Feedback is essential if the participation is going to achieve anything other than informing the public of what is going to happen.

Just knowing the kinds of techniques which are available and their communication characteristics is not enough to actually obtain good public participation. Box 4 has been taken from the *Manual on Public Involvement in Environmental Assessment* produced by the Canadian Federal Environmental Assessment Review Office (FEARO) (1988). This gives guidance on how to plan and implement a public involvement programme to gain the most benefit, and demonstrates that it is an important part of EIA and should be thoroughly planned and phased.

Box 4 The phases of a public involvement plan

Phase 1: Early consultation

This should be as early as possible to identify issues of concern. Companies often try and hide behind confidentiality at this early stage, but they shouldn't as the earlier issues are identified, the easier they are to deal with. An example of the kind of thing that can happen is that a company could make a prediction of the impact on a part of coastline due to an effluent discharge to a river estuary. Observations by the employed consultants could easily miss the fact that the flow rates in the estuary are very low about once in ten years because of a cyclical drought, and thus underestimate the scale of the impact. This is something that a local member of the public is likely to know.

Phase 2: Initial planning

On the basis of the early consultation, detailed preparatory steps are taken leading to the development of a public involvement plan, these are: identifying the decision-making process, identifying the concerned public, identifying the special characteristics of the situation, writing specific objectives and determining information exchange requirements.

Phase 3: Development of action plan

The public participation method to be used is chosen, and very importantly, resources (i.e. money) are committed to the public involvement plan. The activities required in the action plan are scheduled so that meetings are organised and dates publicised in advance.

Phase 4: Implement the plan

The plan is carried out and results are evaluated. At the same time, the effects of the public participation on the project itself in terms of both design and progress are monitored.

Phase 5: Post-decision public involvement

After the project is authorised the liaison established with the public is continued for the duration of the project for further planning, implementation, mitigation, compensation and evaluation of the project. In the event of the project not going ahead, it is important to inform the public of the circumstances for the decision.

Source: FEARO (1998).

1.3.2   Screening

Screening involves a decision about whether a specific action requires EIA. An action could be a development policy, e.g. for transport, or a plan such as the local authority structure plans in the UK, or a programme such as a bypass building programme within a transport policy, or an individual project such as the construction of a power station.

In many countries' procedures, the requirement for EIA applies only to certain projects. The application of EIA at a more strategic level to policies, plans and programmes is a topic which needs much greater consideration, but such a Strategic Environmental Assessment (SEA) is not within the remit of this book.

Not all actions require EIA as this would entail excessive cost and labour. Imagine, for example, the workload created if any house extension was to be subject to EIA. EIA is necessary for actions which are likely to have significant effects on the environment so that the decision-maker has all the necessary information to balance the economic benefits and costs of the development against the environmental benefits and costs. This initial choice as to which action will require EIA is often a highly subjective one and is often (but not always) made by the same people who will use the environmental impact statement later as part of the decision-making process. These people are thus known as the competent authority. They will require basic details about the project and the processes that will be involved, the land use requirements, the infrastructure requirements, raw materials needed, etc.

The screening decision is very important to the developer. If an EIA is required in the UK, the developer will have to pay for the work and will also have to wait until it is completed until the application for planning permission itself will be considered. Because of this, an informal indication from the competent authority that an EIA would be required can frequently lead to design changes at an early stage to reduce the impacts to a level where a formal EIA is no longer required.

As an example, in the UK, the decision as to which projects require EIA is, in most cases, made by the local planning authority which also then determines the planning application upon receipt of the EIS; they are thus the competent authority.

A screening decision can have two outcomes: an EIA either is or is not required. The reasons for the decision in either case can be considered separately.

Possible screening outcomes

EIA is required:

- EIA is mandatory under that country's legislation.

- EIA is not mandatory but public concerns are great.

- Impacts due to the development appear to be significant.

EIA is not required:

- The development is covered by a categorical exclusion in the legislation.

- There is no public concern over a non-mandatory development.

- The mitigation measures designed to alleviate impacts will reduce them to non-significant levels.

Techniques for making a screening decision

Broadly speaking, there are four possible means by which the screening decision is made; these are the use of categorical exclusions, thresholds, discretion of the competent authority, or a combination of these. Each will now be considered in turn:

Categorical exclusions

This relates to projects which in all circumstances will not be subject to EIA. Examples include:

- projects, policies, etc. for reasons of national security (for example, a chemical weapons establishment, despite the associated risks, is frequently exempted from the requirement from EIA by a country's procedures);

- emergency works where action is necessary immediately due to some natural disaster and time obviously cannot be taken to carry out an assessment of the impacts due to those works, e.g. repairs/improvements to storm-damaged flood defences.

Thresholds

Legislation frequently contains a series of thresholds to help with the screening decision. An example using size limits could be that EIA would be required for all housing developments where over 2.5 hectares (ha) of land are used. This type of threshold is inclusive as all projects over the threshold are included. Exclusive thresholds are also used, an example being that no housing developments under one hectare (ha) of land require EIA. With an exclusive threshold, it is implicit that a screening decision has to be made for projects above the threshold.

Discretion

Legislation can leave the screening decision entirely up to the competent authority which will then judge each case on its individual merits.

Combination

Thresholds can be combined with discretion by making EIA mandatory for some projects for which thresholds will be given, and for all others the competent authority will have to use their discretion. This is the approach currently adopted in the UK.

You have to make your own, less formalised, screening decisions at home. Imagine, for example, deciding where to go out in the evenings during a week. You look in a local magazine which tells you 'What's On'. Your choices are: the ballet, an Elton John concert, a football match, a rugby match, a hockey match, the cinema, a live hypnotist. How do you decide what to watch? How do you reach your decision? In reality, you probably don't find the decision that hard to make, but if you analyse it, you may find that it fits into one of the four techniques for screening just discussed.

For example, you may hate pop music and would not go to see a pop concert under any circumstances – even if someone bought you a ticket. This choice for you would be a categorical exclusion.

It may be that you would like to see a ballet just to see what it's like – but at £30 a ticket it's too expensive. This means that it's beyond the threshold of what you would pay. The choices you are left with are affordable and come down to your own discretion. You can see that, in this example, you would have subconsciously used a combination of the available screening methods.

Problems encountered in making screening decisions

Difficulties do remain. For example, in the United States the National Environmental Policy Act (NEPA) 1969, which is the law which requires EIA to be carried out in the US, asks in its section 102(2)C for a detailed statement for "'major' 'Federal actions' 'significantly' affecting the quality of the 'human environment'". This is a short sentence, but it has four undefined terms (in double quotes) which led to a large amount of litigation in the early years of NEPA.

In 1981, 1,033 EISs were filed with the US Environmental Protection Agency (EPA) which receives copies of all EISs produced as a result of NEPA obligations. In the same year, 114 lawsuits were filed, of which 52 claimed that an agency had failed to prepare an EIS where the section 102(2)C sentence quoted above required it to do so. Fifty cases claimed the EIS was inadequate, eight claimed that the EIA itself had been inadequate and the remaining lawsuits were filed on miscellaneous grounds (Canter, 1984).

Quite frequently it is unclear whether the impacts will be significant or not. In the past, the Canadian EIA procedures had a formal matrix approach to overcoming this problem. Once concerns have been identified using a matrix or other approach, how can they be converted into decisions? There are some major criteria which can be applied – magnitude, prevalence, duration and frequency, risks, importance, mitigation, and uncertainty associated with the prediction of impacts (Federal Environmental Assessment Review Office, 1978). These are explained further in section 1.4 which goes into more detail about assessing the significance and magnitude of impacts. Note that these criteria are generally applicable and should not be confused with any specific criteria, such as those contained within UK EIA regulations, which are legally binding.

It must be stressed, however, that where procedures dictate a screening choice based on significance, the decision is a subjective one which depends on the situation. The criteria listed in section 1.4 are the sort of considerations which should be taken into account.

1.3.3   Scoping

Consideration of the issues which should be addressed by an EIA is known as scoping. This term stems from the 1978 regulations (produced by the Council on Environmental Quality) supplementing

NEPA 1969 in the USA which require lead agencies (i.e. the agency with the greatest direct involvement in a particular development – some projects can have several agencies involved) to undertake

> an early and open process for determining the *scope* of issues to be addressed and for identifying the significant issues related to a proposed action.

> (Beanlands, 1988)

The starting point for developers in considering what to cover in an EIA will be the information that is required by the procedures in their country – this is not scoping, it is fulfilling their legal obligations. The developers can, if they wish, cover areas beyond what is legally required if they identify them as important issues. Within these legal constraints, scoping should identify the relevant areas for the development in question, with a view to concentrating resources in these areas.

The need for scoping came about as a result of the large amount of litigation brought about by the vagueness of NEPA 1969. The result, as mentioned earlier, was a strong challenge in the courts on EISs regarding their lack or quality. The effect of this was to cause agencies to produce EISs which covered every conceivable issue, whether significant or not, in minute detail to avoid possible charges of inadequacy. Examples include a 1,980 page EIS for coal-mining in the eastern Powder River Basin of Wyoming in 1975 and a 2,500 page EIS on the Kaiparowits power proposal in Utah in 1976 (Bardach and Pugliaresi, 1977). Hence the requirement for the 1978 regulations produced by the CEQ. These streamlined the process by introducing scoping (absent in NEPA 1969) and limiting the length of EISs to 150 pages, or 300 pages for particularly complex proposals.

What is scoping?

A principal question in scoping is that of significance. In order to address only the important issues in depth, their significance must be assessed and this is where much of the difficulties with EIA lie. In the past, the method of assessing significance frequently involved a conversion to monetary values and a cost-benefit analysis (CBA). This can be useful if carried out correctly. However, all too frequently, a CBA is oversimplistic involving a consideration of market values, so that the cost of a project can be reduced if it uses land which may have low agricultural value and is cheap to buy, even though the same land may be held in high regard for its recreational uses or in terms of its visual or landscape features.

The evolution of an EIA follows the line that social perceptions of concern initially take priority and define the areas where scientific study will concentrate. There then comes a phase when science takes a leading role while an objective study is carried out on the socially recognised concerns. Once the scientific study is completed, the results are made available to the decision-makers on the particular project, at which point social concerns often take priority again.

If the project proceeds, the scientist should again take a leading role as post-implementation monitoring is designed.

What types of scoping are there?

Scoping can be divided into three distinct areas for the purpose of definition: technical, political and social.

- *Technical scoping.* This involves dealing with issues which in the perception of technical experts are important. For example, considering a nuclear power station, a technical expert could identify the disposal of radioactive water as an issue – something which the general public may be unaware of. To carry out technical scoping, consultation with relevant experts would need to take place, including authorities with specific responsibility for some aspect influenced by the project.

- *Political scoping.* This is so named because the decision-makers will have their own priorities, for example the number of jobs created by a particular development. Political scoping should involve consultation with the decision-makers and competent authority staff.

- *Social scoping.* This is the most difficult to deal with as it involves assessing the concerns of the public, thereby requiring comprehensive public particpation.

Social scoping is essential to the smooth passage of a development project through its planning stages to its completion and implementation.

To try and present an everyday perspective on scoping, imagine you are investing in a washing machine. How would you go about deciding which model to buy and why?

You may have suggested obtaining brochures on washing machines from a shop as a first step. These would provide you with technical information about the machines, but really you may have felt that this wouldn't be enough, you would like an assessment of reliability and cost effectiveness. To get this, you might buy a consumer magazine such as *Which?*. The information you would get from such a magazine would be based on public surveys and would, in effect, give the public involvement that you require; it would tell you what to look for, and which features are gimmicks and which are essential. You may even ask neighbours and friends what they think of their washing machines. What you would have done is to scope the issue – you would have found out what are the essential and useful requirements for modern washing machines, and what the public think about the machines on offer.

Assuming that you would go to all this trouble over a washing machine should demonstrate the need for extensive scoping of huge development projects with potentially large effects on the environment and local residents.

1.3.4   Baseline study

After scoping has identified the key issues, the baseline study collects the relevant data to address these key issues. Hence scoping and baseline studies are essentially interrelated. Table 1.1 indicates the sort of information that will commonly be required in a baseline study (note that this is a non-exhaustive list).

It is important to understand that, because of scoping, information will not be needed on each of the headings in Table 1.1, just the relevant ones. Neither is the table all-embracing, it merely lists some of the more common areas which will need examination. It must also be remembered that each project does have some unique features which may require baseline studies of other factors. An example is the development of windfarms. Impacts associated with these developments include visual impact, noise, electromagnetic interference affecting TV reception and shadow disturbance caused by the blades of a wind turbine intermittently blocking out the sunlight as they revolve – possibly causing epilepsy in those who are prone to it (Brooks, 1991). Clearly, a baseline study for a windfarm would require a consideration of the existing landscape, background noise levels, the affected households and the amount of time they would be affected by shadow disturbance, noise and electromagnetic interference.

Table 1.1 Typical baseline study information

Hydrological	• ground water
	• surface water
	• drinking water
	• sewerage
Atmospheric	• sulphur dioxide
	• particulates
	• lead
	• other heavy metals
	• special factors, e.g. radioactive particles
Meteorological	• precipitation
	• temperature
	• wind speed
	• wind direction
	• sunlight duration
	• sea state
Geological	• solid
	• drift
Soils	• types, e.g. using the British soil classification
Land use	• agricultural capability, e.g. using the Ministry of Agriculture, Fisheries and Food (MAFF) agricultural land classification
	• land use types, e.g. agriculture (dairy), residential, heavy industry
Landscape	• classificatory
	• evaluative
Geomorphological	• e.g. man-made spoil tips, river flood plain
Ecological	• habitat
	• flora
	• fauna

To carry out a baseline study, you need to know what is where (spatial information) and how it changes with time (temporal information). If we had a good functional understanding of the system under study, that is to say that we understood the processes that are operating within the system, then we would be in a position to know the period of time over which the temporal information should be gathered and the appropriate area of study.

In many cases, gathering the baseline information may require research to find the current situation and trends. There is, however, a wealth of information readily available if the developer only knew where to go and get it. Table 1.2 lists a whole range of expertise available in the UK for a range of impacts which are laid out according to the requirements for the contents of an EIS in the UK.

Table 1.2 Sources of expertise for baseline studies in the UK

Impact	Sources of expertise
Impacts on human beings:	
Traffic	Local authority Highways Department
Noise	Environmental health officers
	Association of Noise Consultants (http://www.isvr.soton.ac.uk/ANC/)
Litter/dust	Environmental health officers
Socio-economic	Census
Recreational	Local authority Leisure Services Department
	National Parks Authorities
	Ramblers Association (http://www.ramblers.org.uk/)
Flora and fauna	English Nature (http://www.english-nature.org.uk/)
	Countryside Council for Wales (http://www.ccw.gov.uk/)
	Scottish National Heritage (http://www.snh.org.uk/)
	Royal Society for Nature Conservation/local trusts
	Royal Society for the Protection of Birds (http://www.rspb.com/)
	British Trust for Ornithology (http://birdcare.com/birdon/birdaction/bto.html)
	Botanical Society of the British Isles (http://members.aol.com/bsbihgs/)
	British Ecological Society (http://www.demon.co.uk/bes/)
	The Mammal Society (http://www.abdn.ac.uk/mammal/)
	Biological Records Centre (http://mwnta.nmw.ac.uk/ite/eic2.html)
Soil	County minerals officers
	British Geological Survey (http://www.bgs.ac.uk/)
	Soil Survey and Land Research Centre (http://www.cranfield.ac.uk/sslrc/)
	Ministry of Agriculture, Fisheries and Food (http://www.open.gov.uk/maff/maffhome.htm)
	National Farmers' Union (http://www.nfu.org.uk/)
	Royal Agricultural Society of England (http://www.rase.org.uk)
Water	Environment Agency (http://www.environment-agency.gov.uk/)
	Scottish Environment Protection Agency (http://www.sepa.org.uk/)
	Water authorities (Scotland)
	Water plcs and statutory water companies

Table 1.2 (contd)

Air	Scottish Environment Protection Agency (http://www.sepa.org.uk/)
	Environment Agency (http://www.environment-agency.gov.uk/)
	Academic institutions (http://www.scit.wlv.ac.uk/ukinfo/uk.map.html)
	AEA Technology (http://www.aeat.co.uk/netcen/airqual/)
Climate	Meteorological Office (http://www.meto.gov.uk/home.html)
Landscape	The Countryside Agency (http://www.countryside.gov.uk/)
	Countryside Council for Wales (http://www.ccw.gov.uk/)
	Scottish National Heritage (http://www.snh.org.uk/)
	International Centre for Protected Landscapes (http://www.aber.ac.uk/~icpwww/index.htm)
	Council for the Protection of Rural England/Wales (http://www.greenchannel.com/cpre/)
Archaeology	County council archaeologist
	Council for British Archaeology (http://www.britarch.ac.uk)
	Academic institutions (http://www.scit.wlv.ac.uk/ukinfo/uk.map.html)
Cultural assets	National Trust (http://www.nationaltrust.org.uk/)
	Cadw (in Wales) (http://www.castlewales.com/cadw.html)
	English Heritage (http://www.english-heritage.org.uk/)
	Association of Industrial Archaeology (http://www.twelveheads.demon.co.uk/aia.htm)
General	Department of the Environment, Transport and the Regions (http://www.detr.gov.uk/)
	Northern Ireland Environment and Heritage Service (http://www.nics.gov.uk/doehome.htm)
	Institute of Environmental Management and Assessment (http://www.iema.net/)
	Friends of the Earth (http://www.foe.co.uk/)
	Greenpeace (http://www.greenpeace.org/greenpeace.html)
	Council for the Protection of Rural England/Wales (http://www.greenchannel.com/cpre/)
	Civil Aviation Authority (http://www.caa.co.uk/)
	British Wind Energy Association (http://www.bwea.com/)
	Civic trusts
	EIA Unit, University of Wales Aberystwyth (http://www.aber.ac.uk/environment)

A key question the developer will always ask is whether the baseline study is practical. Practicality in this respect can be determined on the basis of costs, logistics and reliability of sampling techniques, as discussed below.

Costs

The costs of data collection are important and can't be ignored. The general perception is, for consultants carrying out the baseline study, to relate its cost to the size of the development. The two should be divorced: it may be the small projects which are already marginal in viability which may cause the biggest environmental problems. Having said that, it would not be possible to saddle high costs on a small developer. In the UK, it could cost a lot of money to get the baseline data needed if it involved a lot of fieldwork. However, it is essential to get all the data that are necessary, even if this means the developer abandoning the project as a result.

Logistics

How feasible is it to collect all the data that is needed? The importance of making measurements over a period of time has already been stressed, and it may be that a period of two years would be ideal for a particular parameter; it is far more likely, however, that a consultant would be given two months. It is essential that a programme of research is derived that is achievable – it may be better to sample intensively for two days to catch any diurnal variations and then increase the timescale.

Reliable sampling techniques

The data collection technique used needs to be consistent, and with technology advancements, data can be collected with data loggers to give a record over time without the sampler having to be there.

Reliable analytical techniques

This can often be a problem with historical data. An example of such a problem arose out of the European Community's drinking water directive (Commission of the European Communities, 1980); this specified that drinking water should not contain any pesticides and placed a limit on nitrates. At the time, analytical techniques were not advanced enough to actually detect the level of pesticides – now they are, but it isn't necessarily the standard of drinking water that has changed because the sensitivity of the analytical technique for detecting pesticides has improved.

Hence if historical data are to be compared with more recent data, the new collection programme should take account of this and try and calibrate the new with the old technique. For example, a past reading of nil pesticides could be changed to <20 ppb (parts per billion).

Example 1 may help you to understand how a baseline study might be planned. Read the brief description in the example of a proposal to extend a waste disposal landfill site and then write down nine possible impacts which you think may have significant effects (i.e. scope the study). For each of these effects, note down just *one* piece of baseline information which you feel it would be necessary to collect before a full impact prediction could be carried out.

1.3.5   Impact prediction

The most efficient way to predict impacts is to first carry out adequate scoping so that the significant impacts have been identified, and resources can then be concentrated on their prediction. Impact prediction usually relies on the existence of models designed specifically for the purpose, for example to predict the effect of producing a certain volume of sulphur dioxide and discharging it at known rates and heights into the atmosphere. These can be purely theoretical, empirical or a combination of both. In some cases, prediction will consist entirely of the opinion of experts – this is especially the case with less quantifiable impacts such as visual intrusion. Frequently, the impact predictions may reveal that the environmental effects are not as great as previously imagined and may not be significant, hence the process can loop back to the scoping phase to amend the EIA accordingly.

Impact prediction is the most scientific part of an environmental impact assessment and careful consideration needs to be taken of the form of presentation of the results if they are to be both comprehensive and understandable to a wide cross section of people. For each of the scoped issues, the impacts need to be predicted in sufficient detail to make the predictions useful. This requires:

- giving sufficient detail to fully explain the impact;

- taking into account each alternative development proposal and site;

Example 1 Application to extend Farrington Road landfill site

The extension to the existing Farrington Road site will provide an extra capacity of 500,000 cubic metres which will be sufficient to meet the landfill needs of the town until 2009. The existing site only has capacity for another six months of operation. The site is predominantly agricultural land and is located 4 km due west of the town centre in a suburban area which comprises a mix of agricultural land, housing, minor industrial developments and a small coal-fired power station.

The site of the extension fringes on a Site of Special Scientific Interest (SSSI), designated for its abundance of dragonfly species which are locally rare. A stream runs through the extension site (it avoids the existing landfill area) and would require culverting. The stream is not used for drinking water.

The major centres of population are to the east and south of the proposed extension site and are on higher land which would overlook the new landfill operation. Refer to Figure 1.7 for a map of the area.

One possible solution to this example can be found in Appendix 2 at the end of the book.

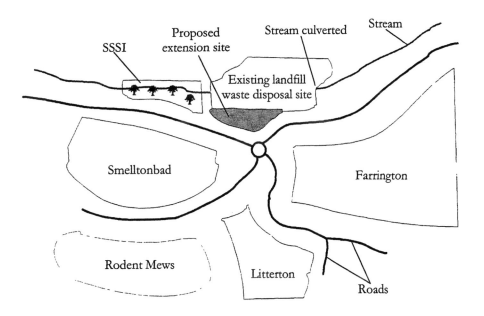

Figure 1.7 Map of Farrington Road landfill site.

- presenting the prediction in a quantified way if at all possible (that is indicating the uncertainty associated with any impact, for example 'there is a 10% chance of all fish life being eliminated');

- giving an appropriate timescale over which the impact can be expected to occur;

- acknowledging alternative views/techniques, if they exist;

- predicting what would happen to the environment in the absence of the development (the 'no-action' alternative).

Example 2 contains two extracts from environmental statements submitted in the UK. It is a valuable exercise at this stage to assess them against the criteria in the list above, and to decide which of the two predictions is more useful. The solution to this example can be found in Appendix 2.

Example 2 Environmental statement extracts

1. 'Extraction will destroy the following features identified in the survey... 1.15 km of moderately species-rich hedgerow: although they are not exceptional, the loss of these hedgerows is in the context of the national picture of 300,000 km lost since 1945.'

2. 'The proposed site has been previously developed and does not support material numbers of birds or mammals. The proposed development will have no impact on the birds and mammals in the areas adjacent to the site.'

Consider the discharge of effluent into a stream. The effect on fish life is one impact which needs to be examined and a suitable prediction would state:

- the percentage drop in fish life as a result of the development;

- what the difference in this prediction would be if the development were at an alternative site;

- what the difference in this prediction would be if the development used a different manufacturing process;

- when the impact would happen;

- likely future trends;

- what the effect on fish life would be if the project did not go ahead (this is known as the 'no-action option').

Impact prediction should not only look for direct impacts, but also indirect impacts and the interactions between them. This is the only way of building up a full picture of the environmental system under study so that the effects can be understood.

1.3.6   Impact assessment

Once predictions have been made about impacts, the essential but difficult task of assessing their importance and significance must be carried out. Only then can a conclusion be drawn.

An impact can appear insignificant if, for example, it would destroy 20% of the habitat for a particular species of amphibian. It may be, though, that the amphibian is globally rare, and that 10% of the habitat in the world is under threat by the development. This will increase the significance of the impact greatly. Conversely, the loss of a pond could be seen as significant as it is the loss of an entire habitat; if, however, the pond is one of 17 in a large field, the significance of the loss wanes considerably. Therefore, it is necessary to collect information on a broader environmental context in order to assess the significance. This means that the study area should extend beyond the development site and its immediate surroundings.

It is this assessment of the impacts which provides the decision-maker with information on the significance of environmental impacts when determining a project application. A good assessment obviously depends on accurate and precise predictions or the uncertainty inherent in those predictions will be reflected in the assessment of significance.

The assessment will form the crucial part of an environmental statement and will need to be able to stand up to the scrutiny of experts, the public, pressure groups and the decision-makers. It can be relied upon that any uncertainty not made explicit in impact predictions will be brought out by one of these groups.

It is important to stress that much of the work in EIA relies on value judgements, and you should always consider who it is that feels an impact is significant and whether a different view is equally plausible.

1.3.7   Mitigation

Mitigation involves taking measures to either reduce or remove identified impacts. It should not be confused with enhancements which are changes unrelated to identified impacts but which improve the environment in some way, for example cleaning up an overgrown and stagnant stream next to a power station and restocking it with fish. This is unrelated to the development and does not address its impacts. It does, however, improve an existing, though unrelated, problem. Examples of mitigation measures include landscaping to reduce visual impact, soundproofing to reduce noise impacts, redesigning a factory process to create less effluent, resiting a car park to save a small section of woodland and building a treatment plant to clean up effluent discharge into a river.

An accurate definition of mitigation is difficult as many different procedures from around the world may have alternative meanings. However, in 1978, the Council on Environmental Quality in the USA produced regulations to complement the world's first EIA legislation – the National Environmental Policy Act 1969. These regulations define what, for the purposes of that Act, is meant by mitigation and the relevant text is reproduced in Box 5.

Box 5 The meaning of mitigation according to CEQ Regulations

(a)   *Avoiding* the impact altogether by not taking a certain action or parts of an action.

(b)   *Minimizing* impacts by limiting the degree or magnitude of the action and its implementation.

(c)   *Rectifying* the impact by repairing, rehabilitating, or restoring the affected environment.

(d)   *Reducing* or *eliminating* the impact over time by preservation and maintenance operations during the life of the action.

(e)   *Compensating* for the impact by replacing or providing substitute resources or environments.

Source: CEQ (1978).

The iterative nature of the EIA process has already been mentioned. The design of mitigation measures provides an opportunity for a developer to use this to their own advantage by, for example, including mitigation measures which reduce impacts to a point where they are no longer perceived to be significant. This can either lead to a reassessment of the need for EIA, with potentially large cost savings for the developer, or a reassessment at the scoping phase to prevent the unnecessary and costly investigation of impacts which have already been designed out of the development.

Impacts which still remain even after the design of mitigation measures are known as residual impacts. These should be stressed so that decision-makers, the public and other interested groups are all well aware of what the actual consequences of the development will be, rather than those predicted prior to mitigation.

An important consideration is how effective the mitigation measures will be – that is, the issue of uncertainty is again an important one. For a mitigation measure which is often used and is highly effective, there can be a high level of confidence that it will achieve its aim. On the other hand, it is important that an assessment of the likely success of new mitigation techniques is made.

Example 3 may help you to understand the potential value of mitigation measures and also help you appreciate exactly what constitutes mitigation. It is a useful exercise to try and think of suitable mitigation measures for the impacts given in this example before turning to Appendix 2 for suggested solutions.

Example 3 Suggesting mitigation measures

1. Visual intrusion at a dwelling resulting from a wind farm 500 m away.

2. Noise due to blasting in a nearby quarry.

3. Increase in bronchitis in people over 60 years old because of a new power station upwind.

4. Increased lead on the grassed recreation area attached to a housing estate due to a new leisure complex attracting more visitors, and hence traffic, to an area.

5. High environmental carbon dioxide levels due to the increase in numbers of motor cars.

1.3.8   The environmental impact statement

The EIS is the report of the environmental impact assessment but it has a number of very important functions to perform:

- It is an aid to decision-making and should therefore provide all the information that the decision-maker will require. The relevant information should have been identified in the scoping stage of the EIA.

- It is a document aimed at informing the public of what is happening and exactly what the development is about. The environmental statement should always contain a non-technical summary so that anyone can understand the research and its conclusions. The public have fears about developments, many of them based on a lack of understanding of what is going to happen. The non-technical summary can help to allay these fears.

- It provides information at a stage early enough to allow experts and concerned organisations to express their views on the development so that the decision-makers have more than just one, potentially biased, view on it.

The content of every EIS will vary, even within one country where they are all subject to the same EIA procedures. The general content should, however, remain similar and would ideally contain all the sections mentioned in Table 1.3.

Producing an EIS is a task that may be taken on by the developers themselves, or may be contracted out to consultants on their behalf. Because of the wide range of different impacts which may have to be investigated, one consultancy may not have all the expertise required to carry out specific research, hence conducting an EIA involves a project management exercise commonly involving one consultancy which subcontracts other specialists.

Table 1.3 Guidelines on the content of an environmental impact statement

Title page
This should contain details of:
* title of the project;
* date;
* the developer responsible for the EIS and the names of any consultancies if applicable;
* the title of the Regulations under which the EIS has been prepared;
* as with any report, a list of contents and references should be included.

Non-technical summary
* The summary should not be lengthy.
* The language should be non-technical.
* It should give an outline of both the project and the location.
* It should focus primarily upon key impacts identified in the EIA and measures taken to avoid or reduce them.
* The alternatives considered should be described briefly along with the rationale for putting forward the proposed project.

Definitions
A set of definitions agreed at the beginning of the EIA process by all stakeholders should be included. This will enable constructive and worthwhile dialogue to take place between the developers and other parties.

Policy, legal and administratuive framework
This is particularly important for those developments which are subject to licensing procedures separate from the decision-making procedure to which the EIA is attached.

Public participation
The public participation that has taken place up to the time when the EIS was submitted should be detailed and should include:
* a description of the nature of the involvement so it is clear how much participation has taken place;
* a description of the timing of involvement;
* an indication of the involvement to take place, if any, after the decision has been taken.

Proposed project
The proposed project should be described in terms that are non-technical, yet still sufficiently detailed to give a full understanding of all the phases of the project. It should include:
* the need for the project;
* the design, size and scale of the project;
* the processes and operations involved in the construction, operation and decommissioning phase;

Table 1.3 (contd)

- the timing and duration of the phases of the project;
- diagrams, sketches or landscape architect's impressions of the project in the receiving environment.

Alternatives

This section should give an account of:

- the alternatives to the project (this may include design, location and strategic options);
- the 'do nothing' option – what will be the outcome of not undertaking the project, on future land use for instance;
- the alternative considered to be the 'most environmentally friendly', if this is not the project;
- the criteria for rejecting the alternatives;
- the stage in the planning process when they were rejected.

Local environment

A description should be given in general terms to indicate the nature and broad character of the local environment. A map(s) should be included and special reference made to:

- adjacent centres of population/proximity to residents;
- designated sites of interest (UK examples are SSSI, AONB, NNR);
- other attributes of the area, e.g. amenity and recreational value.

Site

More information, including a map and photographs, should be provided on the actual site. This should be related to the above. In addition to the aspects covered under the local environment, the site description should include information on:

- the ownership and access;
- the current land use;
- the findings of specific baseline studies.

Method of assessment

This should contain details of the EIA procedure including:

Baseline data:

- what information the EIA was based upon;
- any uncertainties or omissions in this data, e.g. ecological data collected out of season or several years previously;
- any further surveys needed to remedy this.

Consultations: this section should include who has been contacted about the project. It should also include:

- statutory bodies, amenity groups and local residents likely to be affected by the proposals;
- means of contacting them and of providing publicity about the project, e.g. leaflets, public displays, questionnaires, letters, etc.;
- stage in project planning or date when they were contacted;

Table 1.3 (contd)

- a brief summary of their response detailing the areas of concern highlighted and their contribution to the EIA.

EA methodology: if a method other than consultation was used to identify impacts, such as a checklist or matrix, this should be explicitly stated.

Predicted environmental impacts

This section should indicate what effects the proposed development is likely to have on the environment. The EIS should emphasise the key issues identified during the scoping phase and indicate why these are felt to be crucial. Lesser impacts should be mentioned but the amount of space devoted to them should be proportional to their perceived importance.

- Although direct impacts should be the most obvious, indirect and cumulative effects should not be overlooked.
- It should be stated whether impacts are long or short term, whether they are recurrent and whether they are reversible.
- For clarity, impacts may be divided into groups according to the phase in which they occur: construction, operation or decommissioning.
- Where possible, impacts should be quantified and an indication given of both their magnitude and their significance.
- Any uncertainty in the prediction should be made explicit.

Mitigation

For each impact identified, the EIS should state:

- any steps to be taken to avoid or reduce it (mitigation measures);
- the likely success and adequacy of mitigation;
- all residual impacts (those which are unavoidable) should be clearly identified.

Enhancement opportunities

A brief outline should be given of any enhancement work which is planned. This should be distinguished from mitigation measures which are integral to the project and form part of the proposal.

Monitoring

This should indicate:

- the provisions made for the monitoring of all the phases of the development;
- any provisions for audit after completion of the scheme.

Supporting documentation

These will include information which would clutter the main body of the text:

- plans and maps;
- species lists;
- press releases;
- written responses to the project.

Bias of EISs is one of the most common criticisms levelled at EIA, perhaps correctly so. When it is considered that the statements are produced by developers, or by consultants acting under the orders of developers, the reasons for this criticism are all too clear. Frequently, an EIS will promote the good points of a project while glossing over the more unsavoury parts. Once the EIS has been submitted, the decision-maker may not know which facts have been glossed over. A possible solution to this problem, proposed before the UK regulations were introduced, was that EIS preparation should be the responsibility of the competent authority, but that the developer would still pay. This did not happen and within the EU only Denmark has gone down this route.

How can the bias be controlled? The ideal method to control bias is via scoping. If decision-makers themselves or independent groups help to scope the issues for a development, then the contents of an environmental impact statement, and thus potential bias, are controlled to some extent. If a developer has omitted something from the EIS which was originally scoped, the omission could then be picked up by the decision-maker. We will see in a later chapter that scoping by the decision-makers has recently been introduced into the UK EIA regulations (see p. 135).

1.3.9   EIS review

Once the EIS is completed it will need reviewing by the competent authority or other bodies asked to comment on the EIS. It is essential that the statement be checked for consistency, omissions, bias and accuracy. Ideally, review should be independent so that bias can be identified; in some countries' procedures this is facilitated by the use of independent commissions which review EISs (for example the Netherlands – see Wood, 1995).

The purpose of the review is to establish whether the statement provides the necessary information to allow the decision-maker to determine the application. Some form of guidance undoubtedly helps in this process as it will focus the mind of the reviewer on the topics which should be covered by the statement and the level of detail expected.

In the UK, it is possible to determine whether an EIS is procedurally correct, that is that it contains all the information it should in an understandable way, if you have little experience of EIA as review packages do exist. However, such packages cannot test the accuracy of information provided on specific impacts, and there is no alternative to asking a relevant expert to review the information (which can be expensive). The most commonly applied package is known as the Lee & Colley review package after the authors (Lee and Colley, 1992), and has been used frequently in the UK to gauge environmental statement quality. In addition, the Institute of Environmental Assessment based in Lincoln offers a review service based on a package of their own which is a modification of Lee & Colley. Both these packages rely on two users reading through an EIS in detail and reaching a consensus on the score achieved for a series of different categories. From all the scores, an overall quality score can be reached. These packages were originally written for use with the Regulations introduced into the UK in 1988 and are not applicable to the Regulations introduced in 1999. However, at the time of printing, the Institute of Environmental Assessment was in the process of updating their review package, while the Lee & Colley package has already been updated by the Manchester University EIA Centre (see Lee et al., 1999).

The European Commission has also produced review guidance, freely available, which examines EISs to determine their compliance with the Directive (Commission of the European Communities, 1994a).

While these packages provide a useful function for EISs presented in the UK, perhaps the most successful model for EIS review is that used in the Netherlands whereby an independent commission scopes the EIA and draws up guidelines. These same guidelines, which are used by the developer or their consultants, are then used again by the independent commission to review the EIS providing a checklist of information which is expected to be in the document (Wood, 1999). So, a well-documented scoping exercise can provide the basis for effective review and, as the UK is moving towards a more formal scoping stage, the potential is there for improving the effectiveness of the review stage.

1.3.10 Monitoring

Monitoring is an essential component of two stages of the EIA process:

* baseline studies;

* post-development audits

In order that impact predictions can be made, monitoring needs to be carried out to determine the current state of the environment likely to be affected, and also to determine the existing trends in environmental parameters. Likewise, after a development is in place, monitoring needs to take place to determine the accuracy of the predictions and, on a more practical level, to determine compliance with any conditions which may have been set. The key to being able to carry out post-development audits is to have monitoring exercises at the two specified stages which are compatible.

Monitoring should comprise the following (Dipper et al., 1998):

*   recording information about environmental parameters (for example sulphur dioxide concentration) and how they change over time and from place to place;

*   recording information about any impacts which might occur and how serious they are (for example, dead fish seen floating on a river – is it the whole population?);

*   recording information on what caused the impacts (for example, a tank containing chemicals overflowed as it was being filled and the chemical poured into the river) as well as information on the impacts themselves;

*   focusing on environmental parameters more likely to experience serious impacts (for example, if a development is next to a Site of Special Scientific Interest (SSSI) containing rare species then the SSSI needs monitoring).

It is important to realise that monitoring is very closely linked to the post-development audit (PDA). A PDA cannot realistically be carried out unless the monitoring programme has been appropriately planned to record the right kind of data.

1.3.11   Post-development audit/post-project appraisal

A post-development audit (PDA) aims to take data collected via monitoring and compare them with predictions made. Conceptually, then, it is simple. The reasons why we should carry out a PDA are well known. The Economic Commission for Europe (1990) pointed out two functions of EIA which, in their view, were in need of improvement. These were:

- EIA's ability to predict project impacts accurately and convincingly; and

- EIA's capacity to allow project decisions to be made in the absence of certainty about environmental impacts.

They go on to say:

> Concern has been expressed, for example, that EIA analysts lean too heavily on expert opinion when they are making predictions and do not rely enough on empirical evidence from actual projects.

One of the earliest documented PDAs was carried out in 1975 for an off-road motorcycle race across 250 km of the Nevada desert in the USA (Bisset, 1991). The aim was to find out what the impacts were and whether they were sufficiently serious to prevent future races. Some of this study was useful in that it allowed an assessment to be made of the predictions, which in terms of area of land affected and total amount of particulates generated had underestimated the real case. The PDA did, however, demonstrate that insufficient monitoring had been carried out to allow a satisfactory 'before' and 'after' comparison to be made.

This told us, from a very early stage in the development of EIA, that where a PDA is going to be carried out, planning needs to start at the very outset of the EIA so that there will be relevant monitoring data in sufficient quantities to allow conclusions to be drawn.

A more recent study was made of 29 Federal EISs in the USA (Culhane, 1993), the results of which indicated that that one-third of all the data were not auditable. Culhane (1993) also stated that 'the data … are not as quantified and reliable as we would have preferred'.

More recent research relevant to the UK has demonstrated that, based on a study of eight projects, 57% of predictions made in the EISs were auditable and, of these, nearly three-quarters were accurate (Dipper et al., 1998).

1.4 Significance/magnitude

As an EIA progresses, a frequent question which is asked is whether impacts will be significant. For example, at the screening stage it is essential to know this; at the scoping stage, it is necessary to focus on the impacts which have the potential to be significant; the impact assessment stage is all about determining significance. At the same time, we need to know the magnitude of impacts before we can be in a position to determine significance. It is clear, then, that 'significant' and 'magnitude' are important words that we need to understand fully.

Glasson et al. (1994) provide a very simple distinction between the two words which is that magnitude means size, and significance means importance for decision-making (Glasson et al., 1994, p. 114). They also stress that magnitude does not always equate with significance because large changes in environmental parameters due to a proposed development, for example increase in a pollutant to a river, does not necessarily make the water a less suitable habitat or unsuitable for drinking when compared to standards which exist.

A whole chapter in the new *Handbook of Environmental Impact Assessment* has been devoted entirely to 'Criteria and Standards for Assessing Significant Impact' (Sippe, 1999) and anyone wishing to go into this subject in detail would be advised to read this. As necessary context for this book, however, some simple criteria for assessing significance will be presented here.

1.4.1 *Criteria for assessing significance*

Magnitude

This refers to the severity of the impact. For example, if the feeding area of a rare population of geese will be affected, the magnitude will depend on the amount of feeding area affected. If it is 2% it will be a low magnitude impact; if it is 90% it will be high. This criterion should also be looked at in terms of the wider population, so that for a globally rare species, as opposed to locally rare, even a small loss of feeding area has a high magnitude.

Also of importance is the reversibility of the impact. Consider again the feeding grounds of a rare population of geese which comprises mudflats. If the project removes half of the feeding area, but the predicted change in currents would lead to at least an equivalent area of mudflats and hence feeding ground being created, then the impact is of low magnitude, provided that the speed of reversion is fast enough that the population of geese is unaffected.

Prevalence

Is this a one-off project? Often, a project will have a small impact, but there may be concerns that there could be many more such projects in the future leading to a cumulative impact. A typical example of this is a small housing estate: once the development is there, it encourages further house building, and so on... This sort of problem is typical of the UK where each proposal is considered on its individual merits.

Duration and frequency

These criteria are to do with timing:

- Is the duration short or long term? A short-term impact may be a one-off delivery of large materials for construction – it only occurs once and lasts just a day so it is of little concern. If, on the other hand, the project is so large that daily deliveries will be expected for the next three years, then the significance is greater.

- The frequency of an event refers to how often it occurs. For example, if you are a householder living by a railway line with little traffic, say only three trains a day, you would be concerned to discover that a coal-fired power station was going to become operational further along the track which would double the amount of rail traffic going past your house with heavy freight trains. Another example, considering natural systems, could be a river which is subjected to occasional pollution episodes which kill some of the fauna. If the pollution episodes are infrequent, the recolonisation of the fauna might occur quickly meaning that the river system is viable in the long-term. If, however, the pollution episodes are more frequent, then it may be that recolonisation cannot occur. The importance of frequency is clear in this example.

Risks

Risk is defined by Ramsey (1984) as 'a measure of probability of harm occurring in a certain period of time'. Harm could be directed at human beings or other species or environmental systems. It is essential that all risks associated with development are assessed as far as possible and taken into account when considering a planning application. The role of the EIS is to present this information where screening has determined the risks (or other environmental impacts) are significant.

Importance

What sort of importance do we attach to the issue under discussion? Generally, we would be more concerned about a development in a National Park than outside it (unless it affected us directly). Another factor influencing the importance of a proposal would be its national importance. For example, the oil platform developments in the North Sea off the coast of the UK would have been seen as crucial to the economic status of the UK in the past. So an assessment of the importance of a project is a value judgement, and we must appreciate that different sectors of society attach different importance to the same issues.

Mitigation

If the identified problems can be resolved, then there is no problem. An example would be the inclusion of sewage treatment works for a process which would otherwise pollute a water course thus reducing the effects of the proposed process to an acceptable level.

Uncertainty

How likely is it that impacts will occur? How robust are the models to predict the impacts? If the models are not good, then our uncertainty about the outcome is greater and our confidence in the predictions is lower. This needs to be taken into account in the screening decision. For example, it might be that there is a proposal to build a power station on land reclaimed from mudflats. Now it will be possible to predict with 100% certainty that the mudflat habitat will be lost at that locality and the significance of that will be clear. It will also be clear that the proposed power station will emit airborne pollution, for which it is possible to apply air pollution prediction equations in order to predict levels of airborne pollutants like sulphur dioxide at locations around the proposed development. The prediction can be represented as a map with a clear indication of the likely levels of pollutants at ground level averaged over time – but such a map will not be 100% accurate as the actual levels depend on factors such as the meteorological conditions and the production of pollutants in the proposed power station itself. Perhaps the prediction can be made with only 50% certainty? The implication of the uncertainty is that the predicted levels could be higher or lower and, if higher, perhaps there may be health effects or loss of fauna and flora.

It is important to consider, when assessing significance, the relative importance of highly subjective social values and the much more objective results of scientific study. Both are important, but which takes precedence? The role of social and scientific values change throughout an environmental impact assessment in roughly the manner shown in Figure 1.8.

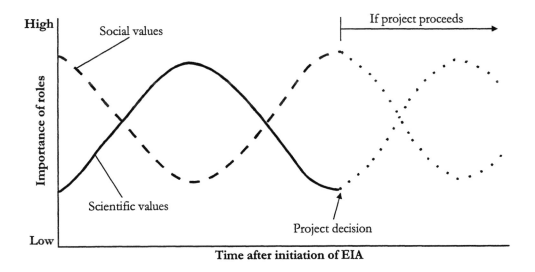

Figure 1.8 The relative importance of social and scientific values.

(Adapted from Beanlands, 1988.)

CHAPTER 2

Where Did EIA Come From?

It is informative to look briefly at the history of EIA because it helps to explain why the process has developed in the way that it has and, more specifically, why so many procedures in place in different countries are so similar.

Table 2.1 indicates the spread of EIA legislation across the world over time based on data collected from a number of sources (Donnelly et al., 1998; Smith and van der Wansen, 1995; Hildén et al., 1998; Kakonge, 1999; Rzeszot, 1999; Briffett, 1999; Brito and Verocai, 1999).

Table 2.1 Spread of EIA legislation across the world

Country name	Legislation year	Country name	Legislation year
Albania	1993	Benin	1995
Angola	Not known	Bhutan	1993
Antarctica	1991	Bolivia	1995
Argentina	1994	Brazil	1986
Armenia	1995	Bulgaria[2]	1992
Australia	1974	Burkina Faso	1994
Austria	1994	Cameroon	1996
Bahamas	1997	Canada[3]	1973
Bahrain	LNI	Cape Verde	1993
Bangladesh	1992	Chile	1991
Belarus	1992	China[4]	1980
Belgium[1]	1993	Colombia	1974
Belize	1992	Costa Rica	1993

Table 2.1 (contd)

Country name	Legislation year	Country name	Legislation year
Croatia[5]	1994	Malta	LNI
Cyprus	1991	Mauritius	1991
Czech Republic	1992	Mexico	1988
Denmark	1989	Moldova	1996
Egypt	1994	Mongolia	1994
El Salvador	1992	Morocco	1996
Estonia	1992	Mozambique	1993
Finland	1990	Namibia	1994
France	1976	Nepal	1997
The Gambia	1988	Netherlands	1986
Georgia	(See Russia)	New Zealand[7]	1974
Germany[6]	1990	Nicaragua	1994
Ghana	1989	Nigeria	1992
Greece	1986	Norway	1990
Guatemala	1990	Oman	1982
Guyana	1996	Pakistan	1983
Honduras	1993	Panama	1991
Hong Kong	1997	New Guinea	1978
Hungary	1993	Paraguay	1993
Iceland	1994	Peru	1990
India	1986	Philippines	1978
Indonesia	1986	Poland	1995
Ireland	1989	Portugal	1987
Israel	1982	Romania	1990
Italy	1988	Russia	1985
Japan	1997	Serbia	1992
Kazakhstan	1991	Seychelles	1994
Korea, South	1981	Singapore[8]	1971
Kyrgystan	1994	Slovak Republic	1994
Latvia	1990	Slovenia	1993
Lithuania	1995	South Africa[9]	1997
Luxembourg	1990	Spain	1988
Madagascar	1991	Sri Lanka	1988
Malawi	1996	Swaziland	1996
Malaysia	1988	Sweden	1991

Table 2.1 (contd)

Country name	Legislation year	Country name	Legislation year
Switzerland	1985	United Kingdom	1988
Taiwan	1994	United States of America	1969
Thailand	1984	Uruguay	1994
Tunisia	1991	Uzbekistan	(See Russia)
Turkey	1988	Venezuela	1976
Turkmenistan	1995	Vietnam	1992
Uganda[10]	1995	Yemen	1990
Ukraine	1995	Zambia	1990

LNI   Law passed but not yet implemented by regulations.

1.   Just for matters covered by Belgium as a whole and not those under the jurisdiction of Flanders, Brussels and Wallonia.

2.   Implementing 1991 Act.

3 .   Canada enacted EIA law in 1995. However, EIA has been operational as an administrative requirement since 1973 according to a government directive.

4.   Regulations were brought in to implement a 1979 Act.

5.   Implementing 1980 Act.

6.   Germany has been carrying out EIA since 1975 but not on a mandatory basis.

7.   New Zealand enacted a new EIA system in 1991.

8.   Although Donnelly et al. (1998) report that EIA has only been carried out formally since 1989.

9.   EIA was first referred to in a 1982 Act but was not legally required until 1997.

10.   Regulations to implement the 1995 law have yet to be implemented.

In compiling Table 2.1 the rationale for placing a year next to a country was that, where legislation has been passed which requires the mandatory implementation of EIA in practice (for some action, whether it be restricted to projects in a particular sector or all encompassing), then the year of that legislation being adopted is listed. It is possible that legislation referring to EIA had been passed years earlier, but has not been implemented by subordinate legislation – the table attempts to report only the year in which EIA was actually implemented on the ground. In many cases the year when EIA became mandatory is a grey area and best guesses have been made, and it is often the case that the source references disagree. A final point is that the existence of legislation does not imply the existence of a functioning EIA system.

If a country is not listed in Table 2.1, it means that the author has found no evidence of a legal instrument being in place to require it, or evidence of policies or administrative procedures for EIA only; this does not mean that EIA definitely does not take place! Indeed, many of the countries not listed will have experience of EIA through the actions of funding banks and may be in the process of developing legislation. In short, Table 2.1 should be referred to for interest rather than as a definitive source as implementation years are subject to interpretation, and you should cross check with the source references to gain a greater insight into what the legislation actually requires. (Letters of complaint about inaccurate entries can be sent to the author but must be supported by justified arguments as to why any listed dates should be changed!)

It is apparent from Table 2.1 that at least 112 countries have some form of mandatory EIA system and that the USA enacted the world's first EIA legislation in 1969; this legislation was the National Environmental Policy Act.

2.1   The development of EIA as a legal process

Thus the legal origin of EIA lies in the USA, and the events leading up to the adoption of the National Environmental Policy Act (NEPA) 1969, the world's first EIA legislation, took place over decades (Wolf, 1983).

The world's first National Park, a landmark in the beginning of the conservation movement, was created on 1 March 1872 when President Grant signed the bill to create Yellowstone National Park. Paradoxically, this was a time in the history of the United States when development occurred very fast leading to a change in the perception that America was a land of limitless space and resources. Through the world wars development continued at a great pace causing concern about the government's role – it seemed clear that development took precedence over the environment. In fact, the same year that Yellowstone became a National Park, Congress also enacted the General Mining Law, still in effect today, which allows unrestricted entry to public lands (for any citizen) to prospect and develop mineral deposits (Smythe, 1997).

Despite environmental disasters such as the Dust Bowl of the USA's Great Plains in the 1930s, it was not until the 1960s that the paradox in the two roles of the government was questioned and emphasis began to shift back towards the environment. A prominent publication in this movement was *Silent Spring* by Rachel Carson in 1963 linking environmental hazards and personal health (Carson, 1963).

The new awareness of the environment culminated in Senator Henry M. Jackson's Committee of Interior and Insular Affairs publishing a report entitled *A National Policy for the Environment* in the summer of 1968. The report was produced by Lynton Caldwell of Indiana University.

A meeting in July 1968 led to the production of a congressional white paper containing possible elements of a national policy on the environment (Andrews, 1976). Then, in February 1969, Senator Jackson introduced the bill. The bill did not declare a national policy or force any actions on behalf of government agencies; it simply established a Council on Environmental Quality (CEQ) which would be an office in the President's Cabinet and would be empowered to commission ecological research.

In May 1969, Jackson introduced an amendment when the bill came back to the house to be approved. The amendment declared a national environmental policy, a statement that each person has a fundamental and inalienable right to a healthful environment, and, most importantly from an EIA point of view, a series of action-forcing provisions including the need for a 'finding' to be produced by the responsible official detailing possible impacts of major actions.

The bill was passed by the Senate and sent to the House of Representatives on 10 July 1969. Before it was discussed by a conference committee in the House, however, Senator Jackson reached a compromise with Senator Edmund Muskie who was promoting a bill for a Water Quality Improvement Act which conflicted with Jackson's bill and had thus led to something of a power struggle between the two senators. The compromise led to an amendment of Jackson's bill, supported by both senators, the most important of which was to substitute the requirement for a 'finding' to the requirement for a 'detailed statement' – the implication being far more emphasis on detail.

The conference committee submitted its report on 17 September and the Senate agreed the bill on 20 December followed by the House of Representatives on 23 December 1969. It became law with Richard Nixon's signature on 1 January 1970 to become NEPA 1969.

2.2   What did NEPA do?

NEPA has undoubtedly been the cornerstone for legislation around the world, much of which has consequently adopted the same problems. NEPA established the CEQ and it also stated general environmental policy. More specifically, section 102(2)C forces action on behalf of the government agencies as it states that:

All agencies of the Federal Government shall –

include in every recommendation or report on proposals for legislation and other major Federal actions significantly affecting the quality of the human environment, a detailed statement by the responsible official on – (i) the environmental impact of the proposed action, (ii) any adverse environmental effects which cannot be avoided should the proposal be implemented, (iii) alternatives to the proposed action, (iv) the relationship between local short-term uses of man's environment and the maintenance and enhancement of long-term productivity, and (v) any irreversible and irretrievable commitments of resources which would be involved in the proposed action should it be implemented. Prior to making any detailed statement, the responsible Federal official shall consult with and obtain the comments of any Federal agency which has jurisdiction by law or special expertise with respect to any environmental impact involved. Copies of such statements and views of the appropriate Federal, State, and local agencies … shall be made available to the President, the Council on Environmental Quality and to the public … and shall accompany the proposal through the existing agency review process.

NEPA 1969 does not specifically mention EIA or environmental impact statements, but environmental impact assessment is what is required by section 102(2)C and the environmental impact statement produced as a result is the 'detailed statement'.

CHAPTER 3

The European Context to the Development of EIA Legislation in the UK

This chapter aims to explain, in broad terms, the way the European Union works and exerts influence over the member states. This explanation is necessary in order to understand the nature of the obligations imposed by the Environmental Assessment Directive on the UK (which is the subject of the next chapter).

3.1 Institutions

The Treaty of Rome 1957 stated that the following four institutions would carry out the tasks of what we now know as the European Union:

- European Parliament;

- European Council;

- European Commission;

- European Court of Justice.

We will look at the composition, functions and powers of each of these in turn. Very briefly, and perhaps too simplistically, the Commission initiates legislation, Parliament comments on it and the Council can reject or adopt it.

3.1.1   European Parliament

The seat of the European Parliament is in Strasbourg and it currently has 626 members, the number coming from each member state being roughly proportional to their population (Germany has 99 members, France, Italy and the UK 87 each, Spain 64, the Netherlands 31, Belgium, Greece and Portugal 25 each, Sweden 22, Austria 21, Denmark and Finland 16 each, Ireland 15 and Luxembourg 6). Each Member of the European Parliament (MEP) is elected by direct universal suffrage, meaning that elections are held in which the members are voted in directly in each of the member states. Before 1979, however, the governments of the member states used to appoint the Members of the European Parliament.

The European Parliament has a very important role in the affairs of the European Union but, traditionally, has lacked real power. The one exception to this has been that the Parliament does have the power to compel the European Commission to resign as a body (i.e. all the Commissioners must resign) with a two-thirds majority vote (Article 144 of the Treaty of Rome). Some of these 'no confidence' proposals have been tabled, but none has been successful (Anon., 1989). The entire executive of 20 Commissioners did resign on 16 March 1999, but this was not as a result of the European Parliament compelling them to do so (although press coverage at the time makes it clear that the Commissioners would have been compelled to resign had they not taken the decision themselves – see *The Times*, 16 March 1999). The Amsterdam Treaty 1997, which was ratified in 1999 and came into force on 1 May 1999, has extended the powers of the European Parliament.

The Parliament has the right to set up standing and temporary committees. At the present time (as of 28 June 1999), there are 20 standing committees, one of which covers the environment (Committee on the Environment, Public Health and Consumer Protection). The Parliament has some very important functions that help keep track of the activities of the European Commission and the European Council. Some of these are the right to ask questions, their consultative function and their powers over the budget. These will be considered in turn.

Members of the European Parliament can ask questions of the Commission and the Council. There is then a specified period in which a reply has to be given. The questions can be in either written or verbal form, but the pressure of time means that the majority are written questions and answers that are published in the *Official Journal of the European Community*. In 1985, a total of 4,599 questions were asked of both institutions (Anon., 1989). This is important for EIA as citizens of EU countries can request their MEPs (Members of the European Parliament) to ask a question directly to the European Commissioner in charge of EIA to alert them of something perceived to be going wrong in a member state with the EIA procedure. Ultimately, such questions can lead to the Commission investigating the implementation of a Directive in member states and, in some cases, can lead to European Court action against that member state.

The European Parliament has traditionally been asked to comment on proposals put forward by the Commission before the Council makes a decision on the final text. A change to this traditional procedure was introduced by the Single European Act that amended the Treaty of Rome in 1986. This led to what is known as the cooperation procedure whereby the Parliament's opinion has to be considered by the Commission and the Council before a decision is made. The cooperation procedure, however, is only carried out for some policy areas, such as freedom of establishment and regional policy, and the environment. The steps involved in these two procedures are illustrated in Table 3.1.

There are two others possible procedures for approving legislation: the co-decision procedure (which involves three readings of the legislation) and the assent procedure. Which of these is actually used depends on which article of the Treaty of Rome (as amended by later Acts such as the Single European Act) the legislation in question is based on.

The co-decision procedure involves the Parliament sharing decision-making power equally with the Council. If the Council fails to take due account of the Parliament's opinion in its common position, the Parliament can prevent the adoption of the proposal. If the Parliament decides to reject the proposal the Council cannot adopt it. To prevent this situation from arising, a conciliation committee (made up of Members of Parliament, the Council and the Commission) is convened to seek a compromise before the Parliament's third reading. If agreement is still not reached, the Parliament can reject the proposal definitively. This co-decision power, along with the assent procedure, is at present one of the Parliament's most important powers. Since ratification of the Amsterdam Treaty 1997, the co-decision procedure now applies to most areas of EU legislation.

Table 3.1 Procedures for adopting legislation

Traditional procedure	*Cooperation procedure*
1. A proposal is presented to the Commission who considers it and forwards it to the Council if it has merit.	1. The Commission formulates a proposal and passes it to Parliament and ECOSOC.
2. The Council refers the matter to Parliament and to the Economic and Social Committee (ECOSOC).	2. Parliament and ECOSOC pass an opinion back to the Commission.
3. The Parliament debates the matter, votes and passes an opinion back to the Council. ECOSOC passes its opinion back to Council.	3. The Commission passes the proposal and opinion on to the Council who adopt a common position by a qualified majority. The matter is is then referred back to Parliament.
4. The opinion of Parliament is not binding on the Council. The matter is referred to any relevant committees and then to the Committee of Permanent Representatives (COREPER) who are nominees of the governments of the member states. They act on the instructions of their governments and settle any outstanding matters before referring the matter back to a Council meeting.	4. Parliament have three months to either: (a) approve the Council's position who will then adopt the Act; or (b) reject the Council's position which the Council must act unanimously to overturn; or (c) amend the Council's position by an absolute majority of its members which means that the matter is referred to the Commission.
5. A decision is taken.	5. The Commission has one month to review Parliament's amendments and can then revise their proposal. If they do, the matter is referred back to the Council.
	6. The Council can either: (a) adopt the proposal by qualified majority; or (b) adopt Parliament's amendments which have not been approved by the Commission unanimously; or (c) amend the Commission's proposal unanimously; or (d) fail to act in which case the proposal lapses.

Under the assent procedure, the Parliament's assent is now needed for, among other things, decisions on the accession of new member states.

The European Parliament has complete control over 30% of the budget of the EU: that related to administration and operational expenditure. Parliament can also propose modifications to the rest of the budget which are deemed to be accepted unless the Council rejects them by qualified majority (a term which will be explained in our look at the European Council below). Further to this, they have the power to reject the budget entirely, a power that they have in the past exercised (for the 1980 draft budget).

3.1.2   European Council

The European Council is the legislative body of the EU. It consists of 15 national government representatives that, for the day-to-day running of the EU, are normally the foreign ministers of the member states. For more specific matters, the appropriate ministers attend, for example environment ministers or agriculture ministers. The presidency of the Council rotates on a six-monthly basis between all of the member states. Holding the presidency simply means that the member state must coordinate and preside over the meetings which can take place anywhere in the EU (but usually take place in Brussels).

The Council produces regulations and directives that are the main legal instruments of the EU. To do this, the Council of Ministers must vote on a proposal. This used to require unanimity in most cases, but it meant that the process of producing regulations and directives was extremely slow and now *qualified majority* voting is commonly, but not universally, used. In this system, there is weighting of votes as shown in Table 3.2.

A qualified majority requires 62 votes. This ensures that larger states cannot coerce smaller states (Germany, France, Italy, the UK and Spain acting together still don't have 62 votes). Unanimity is still required for important matters, such as the admission of a new member into the Union, adopting new legislation which has been amended from the form submitted by the European Commission, or legislation brought under Article 100 of the Treaty of Rome.

Table 3.2 Weighting system for qualified majority voting

Member states	No. of votes
Germany, France, Italy, United Kingdom	10 each
Spain	8
Belgium, Greece, the Netherlands, Portugal	5 each
Austria, Sweden	4 each
Denmark, Ireland, Finland	3 each
Luxembourg	2
Total	87

3.1.3   European Commission

The European Commission comprises 20 *Commissioners* (these are individual people) and 26 *Directorates General* (these are similar to departments and are run by lots of people answering to the Commissioners). The United Kingdom, France, Germany, Italy and Spain all provide two Commissioners (because of their larger size/populations) and the other member states one each.

Commissioners are appointed by agreement between the governments of the member states for a term of five years each, which is renewable. During those five years, the Commissioners cannot be removed from office except by a vote of the European Parliament as discussed earlier. Significantly, the Commissioners cannot be removed from office by their own national governments as they are supposed to be independent. Some national governments have felt that their Commissioners have been too independent and have refused to reappoint them at the end of their five-year term. One of the 20 Commissioners can be elected as a President for a term of two years (renewable) by the mutual agreement of the member states.

The Directorates General have responsibilities in specific areas, for example DG XI (Directorate General 11) has responsibility for the environment. It is the DGs which produce the draft legislation in their specific area of expertise. DG XI had personnel numbering around 150 in 1990 compared to total personnel numbering around 15,000 in the Commission at the same time (the Commission employed 19,000 officials in 1994). Their budget was 55 million euros out of a total Commission budget of 55 billion euros. To put their understaffing into perspective, the UK Department of the Environment employed about 2,000 officials and the US Environmental Protection Agency employed about 15,000 officials at the same time (Kramer, 1992).

As well as their function in formulating legislation, the Commission also has the task of ensuring that the rules of the Union are respected and applied properly. This includes forcing member states to implement Directives fully. The Commission has powers, under Article 169 of the Treaty of Rome, to ensure that member states follow the rules. These powers are divided into three stages as follows:

1.   This is the informal stage where the Commission writes to a member state allowing it an opportunity to comment on the violation.

2.   This is the reasoned opinion stage where the Commission issues a document to the member state stating that it is in violation of Treaty of Rome obligations and where this violation has occurred. The member state is then given a period of time in which to respond.

3.   If the member state fails to comply, the Commission brings the matter before the European Court of Justice.

3.1.4   European Court of Justice

The European Court of Justice sits in Luxembourg and comprises 15 judges assisted by nine advocates-general. Their appointment is by mutual agreement between the governments of the member states and is for six years.

The advocates-general make reasoned submissions in open court which provide the basis of facts and legal arguments on which the judges can make a decision.

The European Court of Justice is the highest court in Europe and has jurisdiction over disputes which may arise between the institutions, between member states, between the institutions and member states, and between the institutions and private parties.

The Treaty of Rome 1957 has four important articles that enable the Court of Justice to enforce Union legislation.

Article 169

This has already been discussed in the context of the Commission's role in ensuring compliance with the laws of the EU. The article states:

> If the Commission considers that a Member State has failed to fulfil any of its obligations under this Treaty, it shall issue a reasoned opinion on the matter after giving the State concerned the opportunity to submit its comments.

> If the State concerned does not comply with the terms of such opinion within the period laid down by the Commission, the latter may bring the matter before the Court of Justice.

Article 170

> Any Member State which considers that another Member State has failed to fulfil an obligation under this Treaty may bring the matter before the Court of Justice.

> Before a Member State institutes, against another Member State, proceedings relating to an alleged infringement of its obligations under this Treaty, it shall bring the matter before the Commission.

> The Commission shall deliver a reasoned opinion after the States concerned have been given the opportunity both to submit their own cases and to reply to each other's case both orally and in writing...

Article 171

> If the Court of Justice finds that a Member State has failed to fulfil any of its obligations under this Treaty, such State is bound to take the measures required for enforcement of the judgement of the Court.

Article 177

The Court of Justice shall have jurisdiction to give preliminary rulings concerning…the validity and interpretation of measures taken by the institutions of the Community…

Where such a question is raised before any court or tribunal of one of the Member States, that court or tribunal may, if it considers that a decision on the question is necessary to enable it to give judgement, request the Court of Justice to give a ruling thereon.

Where such a question is raised in a case pending before a court or tribunal of a Member State, from whose decisions there is no possibility of appeal under internal law, that court or tribunal shall be bound to bring the matter before the Court of Justice.

(European Economic Community, 1967)

3.2   Legal hierarchy within European Union member states

Within any country or confederation of countries, legislation can be split into at least two groups: *primary* and *secondary*. The primary and secondary legislation of the European Union will be considered here and will be followed by an explanation of the obligations they impose on member states like the United Kingdom.

3.2.1   *Primary legislation*

These are the treaties that established the EU and state its policies. The very first piece of primary legislation within the EU was the Treaty of Rome 1957. This has been amended by Treaties of Accession which allow new members to join, and by amending Acts such as the Single European Act 1986, the Treaty on European Union 1992 (more commonly known as the Maastricht Treaty) and the Amsterdam Treaty 1997.

Member states, in general, have produced their own primary legislation which 'gives effect' to the EU treaties, acknowledges their superior status and implements them into domestic law.

3.2.2   *Secondary legislation*

This is a collective term for all the legislation produced by the Commission and the Council. This legislation is subordinate to the treaties on which they are based. This means that they cannot amend a treaty, and cannot implement provisions which are not in accordance with the treaties. Another way of looking at this is that the primary legislation states principles which will be implemented by secondary legislation. It is the secondary legislation which forces actions within the member states. Secondary legislation is sometimes called delegated legislation as the authority to produce it is delegated to institutions within the EU, or to an individual ministry within a member state.

What this means is that the institutions of the EU can only act within a remit given to them by the member states themselves in the form of treaties. This situation has come about because of the understandable reluctance of the member states to pass over their sovereignty.

Article 189 of the Treaty of Rome states the following:

> In order to carry out their task and in accordance with the provisions of this Treaty, the Council and the Commission shall make regulations and issue directives, take decisions, make recommendations or give opinions.

> A regulation shall apply generally. It shall be binding in its entirety and take direct effect in each Member State.

> A directive shall be binding, as to the result to be achieved, upon each Member State to which it is directed, while leaving to national authorities the choice of form and methods.

> A decision shall be binding in its entirety upon those to whom it is directed.

> Recommendations and opinions shall have no binding force.

> (European Economic Community, 1967)

Each of these forms of secondary legislation will be considered in turn.

Regulations

These apply in every member state either on a date specified within them or on the twentieth day following their publication. They have the following four characteristic features (Anon., 1989).

1. They are of general application. This means that they do not apply to a limited number of persons or to an individual case, but to categories of persons or situations defined in a general way.

2. They are binding in their entirety. This means that a member state must implement exactly what the regulation states. There is no scope to interpret them and achieve their aims by other means.

3. They are directly applicable, i.e. they are incorporated automatically into the law of the member state. It is normally automatically implemented, although this depends on the nature of the regulation; if they require the imposition of levies, then the member state would be required to adopt legislation to implement the regulation in full.

4. They are applicable in all member states.

An example of a regulation is Regulation 1210/90 which set up the European Environmental Agency.

Directives

Treaties can be indirectly implemented by means of directives. These require the member states to use their own legislative powers to achieve a specified goal. Thus, a directive is binding on a member state in terms of the result to be achieved, but the means by which the result is achieved is left up to the member state. Unlike regulations, directives don't give rights to individuals, but where a directive is not implemented within the time limit specified in the directive for compliance, then individuals may acquire rights. This point will be discussed more fully in a later section.

An example of a directive other than that on Environmental Assessment is Directive 76/160 on the quality of bathing water. The majority of EU environmental legislation is in the form of directives rather than regulations.

Decisions

Decisions issued by the European Council have binding force on the parties involved, whether they are member states, organisations, firms or individuals.

Recommendations and opinions

It is also possible for the institutions to make recommendations and give opinions, but these are not binding.

Drafting a directive

The original text of a directive will be prepared by the relevant Directorate General of the European Commission which assembles the available data. Consultation can then take place with other departments within the Commission, and then with the member states themselves. Once the draft text has been taken through these stages by the relevant Commission department, a *draft proposal* is produced which is then the subject of multilateral discussions between the department and the 15 member states in Brussels.

This stage can be relatively fast, with only a few multilateral meetings required. Alternatively, it can take a long time if many problems are identified – the 1985 Environmental Assessment Directive had 23 different proposals drafted before the text could become an official proposal for a directive (Kramer, 1992).

The next stage, once a text has been approved by the consultation procedure, is for the text to go back to the Commission to start the formal adoption phase. Any remaining differences are settled within the 20 members of the Commission, at which point the text becomes an official Commission proposal for a directive and is published in the *Official Journal of the European Communities (OJ)*.

The proposal for a directive then follows one of the procedures that have already been explained in section 3.1.1 of this chapter. This also applies for amending an existing directive.

3.3   Supremacy of Union law

Quite simply, European Union law takes precedence over the national laws of the member states. As a result, it is not legal for a member state to introduce legislation that is at odds with European Union legislation. This fact has been established via case law in the European Court of Justice. The very first case that established the primacy of Union law was the *Costa* v. *Ente Nationale per l'Energia Electrica* (ENEL) in 1964. In this case, an individual claimed before his local court in Milan, Italy, that the law nationalising the production and distribution of energy was incompatible with the Treaty of Rome. The local court referred several questions to the European Court of Justice for a ruling. The view of the Italian government at that time was that they were perfectly entitled to apply the nationalisation law as it postdated the EEC Treaty and the principle of *implied repeal* would apply, meaning that any legislation which is passed by a government amends earlier laws which are inconsistent with it.

The Union would not be able to function as intended if national laws could be passed which had primacy over European Union laws. As a result, the European Court of Justice found that

> it is impossible for the States to set up a subsequent unilateral measure against a legal order which they have accepted on a reciprocal basis.

The Court found that primacy of EU law was guaranteed by Article 189 of the Treaty of Rome and after some other points went on to state:

> It follows from all these observations that law stemming from the Treaty, an independent source of law, could not, because of its special and original nature, be overridden by domestic legal provisions, however framed, without being deprived of its character as a Community law and without the legal basis of the Community itself being called into question. The transfer by the States from their domestic legal system to the Community legal system of rights and obligations arising under the Treaty carries with it a permanent limitation of their sovereign rights against which a subsequent unilateral act incompatible with the concept of the Community cannot prevail.

A case was brought before the European Court of Justice in 1991 that established, once and for all, the supremacy of EU law over UK national law. This was *Factortame Ltd* v. *Secretary of State* (1991) concerning the legality of the UK Merchant Shipping (Registration of Fishing Vessels) Regulations 1988. These stated that vessels can only be entered onto the register of British vessels if their owners are British citizens or domiciled in Britain. The concern of the UK government at this time was quota hopping as Spaniards would register their vessels on the British register to get some of the British quota of fish. The European Court of Justice held that a national court may set aside an Act of Parliament, or delegated legislation, pending a decision on its validity as a matter of EU law. In this case, the regulations were inconsistent with the fundamental freedom of the Union.

This was a landmark case in the United Kingdom as it was the first time that an Act had gone through both the Houses of Parliament and Lords and then not ended up as irrefutable law.

How can European Union Law take precedence over UK law? When a country joins the European Union, they have to change their own laws so that it becomes clear that EU law is recognised and that it takes precedence over national laws. The European Communities Act 1972 is a UK Act of Parliament which provides that EU law is recognised as law in the UK in its section 2(1).

The United Kingdom has primary and secondary legislation in the same way that the European Union has. In the UK, an Act of Parliament would be classed as primary legislation but, typically, this legislation does not actually force changes in the law as it tends to discuss in broad terms the desired outcome – it is the secondary or delegated legislation which performs this task by setting out specific procedures to be followed to achieve the aims of the primary legislation.

3.3.1   Direct applicability and direct effect

What do the terms in this heading mean? Direct applicability means that a provision of European Union law becomes part of the national law of a member state without the need for further legislation. Direct effect means that a provision of Union law can create rights which individuals may enforce against the state, or in some circumstances against other persons. These meanings will be explained more fully in the following discussion which will look at the direct applicability of regulations and directives separately.

Regulations

Article 189(2) of the Treaty of Rome states that 'A regulation shall have general application. It shall be binding in its entirety and directly applicable in all Member States.' Hence it is directly applicable and can have both *horizontal direct effect* and *vertical direct effect*. The distinction between these two types of direct effect is that vertical direct effect imposes obligations on the state and gives an individual rights to take the state to court where it has not fulfilled an obligation under EU law. Horizontal direct effect imposes obligations on individuals and gives an individual rights to take another individual to court where they have not fulfilled an obligation under EU law.

Directives

These are not directly applicable because the choice of form and methods used to achieve a set aim is left to the member states. They have, however, been found to be capable of vertical direct effect. That this is so was established by a case brought before the European Court of Justice in 1974. The case, *Van Duyan* v. *Home Office* (1974), was brought under Directive 64/221 (Freedom of Movement of Persons within the Community) which the UK government had not implemented within national law. The UK Home Office would not let Ms Van Duyan, a Dutch citizen, into the UK to work on the grounds that she was a member of the Church of Scientology. The European Court of Justice held that conditions for direct effect were satisfied as the provisions (i.e. the directive) were sufficiently clear, precise and unconditional that the lack of member state's implementing legislation did not matter. This case is clearly demonstrating vertical direct effect because the individual was able to enforce an obligation on the state. The UK was obliged to implement the directive on freedom of movement of persons within the Community, and the fact that they had not did not make their subsequent action legal.

What about horizontal direct effect? European case law has shown that a directive is not capable of horizontal direct effect. The case which proves this is *Marshall* v. *Southampton Area Health Authority* (1986). This was a case brought under Directive 76/207 (Equal Treatment Directive). Mrs Marshall challenged her employer, the Southampton Area Health Authority, on the grounds that its differential compulsory retirement ages for men and women was in breach of Directive 76/207. The European Court of Justice ruled that it was in breach of the directive but it noted that the directive could not be invoked directly against an employer – only against the state. The question of what exactly constitutes an emanation of the state was not defined.

3.3.2   The development of EU environmental policy

To provide a good background to the introduction of the Environmental Assessment Directive in 1985, it will be helpful to examine the development of EU policy on the environment. This section aims to do this. The Union does, now, aim to protect the environment and gives it a high profile. This has been demonstrated by case law. In 1989, the case of *Commission* v. *Denmark* (1989) was brought before the European Court of Justice. This case has come to be known as 'the Danish Bottles Case'. Under Danish law, beer and soft drinks containers had to be returnable. The Commission argued that this was an impediment to free trade under Article 30 of the Treaty of Rome. Denmark argued the environmental protection aspects of their law as a defence. The European Court of Justice ruled that it was permissible to use environmental protection as an excuse.

This case is important, as it was the first occasion on which the environment was seen to take precedence over trade. The European Court of Justice stated that the protection of the environment was one of the EUs 'mandatory requirements'. This was not always the case, as we shall see.

Inception of policy

Originally, there was no environmental policy in the Treaty of Rome 1957. In fact, the Treaty did not contain the word 'environment' at all. Later on, the approximation of economic policies of the member states was taken to include environmental issues, the feeling being that divergent national policies on the environment might lead to a distortion of fair competition by increasing production costs in some member states.

From 1973, the EU began to set out policies on the environment by means of their action programmes. These were not law, but statements of intent for the future. Thus the action programmes set out the Union's aims for the environment. In the early years, such policy concentrated on 'clean-up' measures to reduce pollution and improve certain aspects of the environment. However, the second and third action programmes have led to a change of emphasis to protection of the environment and preventing pollution.

The action programmes to date have been:

First action programme for the environment	1973 – 1976
Second action programme for the environment	1977 – 1981
Third action programme for the environment	1982 – 1986
Fourth action programme for the environment	1987 – 1992
Fifth action programme for the environment	1993 – 2002

Problems with implementing EU legislation on the environment

To force action on the environment, some form of legislation is required in terms of secondary legislation, i.e. regulations or directives. To produce secondary legislation, the necessary power is required from the primary legislation, i.e. the Treaty of Rome 1957. The articles of this Treaty which were used to produce regulations and directives concerning the environment, prior to its amendment by the Single European Act in 1986, were Articles 100 and 235.

Article 100 empowers institutions (Council, Commission, Parliament) to 'issue directives for the approximation of such provisions laid down by law, regulation or administrative action in Member States as directly affect the establishment or functioning of the common market'. Hence this article was used for directives on pollution control and common standards, for example harmonising the exhaust emission standards for cars.

Article 235 states that 'if action by the Community should prove necessary to attain, in the course of the operation of the common market, one of the objectives of the Community, and this Treaty has not provided the necessary powers…' Hence this article can be used to produce secondary legislation with a purely environmental content, for example the Wild Birds Directive 79/409.

Directives have been based on either or both of these articles in the past. Whatever the basis, unanimity was always required in the Council before it could be adopted. It is also an important point that environmental legislation could not be imposed in the form of regulations, only directives under Article 100 and, although regulations were possible under Article 235, they were seldom used (Kramer, 1992).

The Single European Act 1986

The Single European Act introduced Title VII into the Treaty of Rome which set out the Commission's policy for the environment, roughly similar to the policies set out in the Union action programmes.

The Single European Act introduced explicit environmental law-making powers in Articles 130r, 130s and 130t. It also amended Article 100 with Article 100a so that environmental legislation had a more legally sound basis. Before this amendment, it was always possible that a member state in disagreement with an environmental directive could have taken the European Commission to court claiming that it had acted beyond the powers given to it by the Treaty of Rome in formulating such legislation. In practice, this did not happen because all environmental directives and regulations under Articles 100 and 235 had required unanimity within the Council of Ministers to be passed.

The importance of these additional articles is not purely that they provide an environmental basis for legislation, but also that, under Article 130s, there is provision for voting by qualified majority if the Council unanimously decides that it would be appropriate (this might, for example, allow more stringent legislation to be passed than would be possible where unanimity were required). Article 100a provisions can be adopted using qualified majority voting where aspects of health and human life are being considered (Kramer, 1992).

To summarise the changes made by the Single European Act, Kramer (1992) has explained the current arrangement for basing directives on articles of the amended Treaty of Rome as opposed to the previous practice. This is shown in Table 3.3.

Table 3.3 Diagrammatic model for basing directives on
Treaty articles

Arrangement prior to Single European Act	Present arrangement
Article 100	Article 100a
Article 235	Article 130s(1)
Articles 100 and 235	Article 130s(2)

Source: Kramer (1992).

CHAPTER 4

What Does the EU Directive on EIA Specify?

4.1 Directive 85/337/EEC

The European Union adopted the first directive on Environmental Assessment in 1985 (European Council, 1985). This was recently amended in March 1997 (European Council, 1997). This chapter will look at the obligations imposed by both of these in turn. The reasons for this are twofold:

- The original directive has shaped European legislation to date.

- The majority of environmental statements in circulation in libraries, with local authorities, with developers and consultants and elsewhere will have been written to meet the obligations of the 1985 Directive. (Based on current environmental statement production rates indicated in Bellanger and Frost (1997) it is likely to be around 2009, give or take a few years, before environmental statements submitted in the UK under the new regulations implementing the 1997 Directive outnumber those submitted under the regulations implementing the 1985 Directive.) Hence it will be useful to know what these obligations were.

The new directive, amending the previous one, was supposed to be implemented within member states by 14 March 1999.

The title of the 1985 Directive is: 'Council Directive on the Assessment of the Effects of Certain Public and Private Projects on the Environment (85/337/EEC)'. For simplicity, it is known as the Environmental Assessment Directive. The code at the end of the title is something you will find for every directive. The first part is the year in which it was adopted, the second part is the number which is simply a sequential number for the directive being adopted during that year, and the final part shows that it is a European Economic Community directive (before the name changed to the European Union).

The form of the Environmental Assessment Directive is quite important. It contains:

- a preamble;

- 14 articles;

- annexes.

Remember that, being a directive, member states are obliged to implement measures that will achieve the aims of the directive, but they do have the right to go further and implement more stringent measures. This is not always as simple a step as it seems. If we take the example of the United Kingdom, when the country joined the EU, an Act of Parliament was required to give authority to EU law. This Act, the European Communities Act 1972, also gave the Secretary of States the power to produce secondary legislation to implement directives, but in doing so, there is no authority for a Secretary of State to go further than is required by the directive. It would take another Act of Parliament to allow this to happen.

What we will do in this section is to go through the directive, looking at the implications of each of its parts. Figure 4.1 has been included to help in this task. It will be useful to refer to this as you read through this section. It is a flow chart that indicates the obligations that the directive places on the member states in drawing up their national EIA legislation.

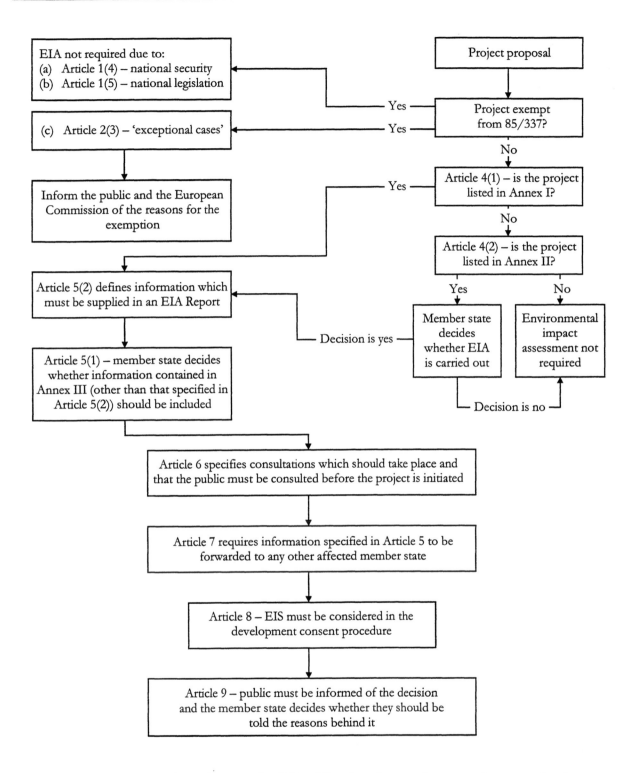

Figure 4.1 Flow chart showing the EIA obligations imposed on member states by the Environmental Assessment Directive.

4.1.1   Preamble

This is the first part of the directive, preceding the articles.

All the preamble does is set the background for the directive. The original proposal for the directive would have come from the European Commission, and opinions would have been given on the proposal by both the European Parliament and the Economic and Social Committee. The preamble states this, and that the directive is a measure in line with the Community action programmes on the environment. It is also stated that the directive is based on both Articles 100 and 235.

The main principles involved in environmental assessment are then outlined:

- environmental assessment should be introduced for private and public projects likely to have significant effects on the environment;

- development consent will require possession of the environmental assessment information where it is appropriate to carry it out;

- there are separate categories of projects: those which will always require environmental assessment and those for which environmental assessment will only be required at the discretion of the member state;

- environmental assessment is necessary to take account of human health, to lead to a better environment and to ensure species diversity.

The preamble ends by allowing exclusions from the procedures it is about to outline where a project is approved by an act of national legislation or in other cases where sufficient reasons are then given to the European Commission afterwards.

The last exclusion allows for emergency works where there clearly isn't time to go through the lengthy process of an environmental assessment, for example works to prevent flooding. The directive states in the preamble that it accepts that such works can go ahead without an environmental assessment, but the case must be justified to the European Commission after the event.

4.1.2　Articles

These are the main parts of the directive which state what must be achieved and implemented by the member states.

Article 1

The first part of this article is the important one. It states that EIA will be carried out on public and private projects. This differs from NEPA in the United States that only applies to public projects. The article goes on to define the terms project, developer and development consent, and indicates that each member state has to designate bodies to have jurisdiction over the EIA process. Unfortunately, the most important term, 'significant', is not defined.

The final parts of the article indicate that projects serving national defence purposes aren't covered by the directive, presumably for secrecy reasons, and reiterates the preamble in that the directive doesn't apply to projects adopted by acts of national legislation. A project that would fit into this category would be the Channel Tunnel in the UK, but an EIA was carried out in this case.

Article 2

Member states have to make sure that environmental assessment is performed on all projects that are likely to have significant effects on the environment. The most important things to consider in deciding this are the size, nature and location of the project. The term *inter alia* means 'among other things' so we know that the decision is not made on the basis of these three points alone.

Member states are told they have to comply with the directive and that, where they do not, they must justify their reasons to the European Commission.

Article 3

This article is concerned with the general scope of the directive and lists a few items that should be considered in an EIA. Unfortunately, the article does not define exactly what is meant by the terms, for example, 'cultural heritage'.

Article 4

This article introduces a distinction between projects that are listed in Annex I and those listed in Annex II. Projects listed in Annex I must always be subjected to EIA. Thresholds for the size of a project that make its effects significant are contained within this Annex (these projects will be discussed in more detail on pp. 83 and 86).

Projects listed in Annex II must be subjected to EIA only where the member state considers that its characteristics require it (these projects will be discussed in more detail on pp. 83 and 86).

This division of projects, subject to EIA, into a mandatory and a discretionary annex gave great scope for the requirement for EIA to vary greatly across Europe. All member states will have to require EIA of projects in Annex I, but their requirements for EIA of projects in Annex II can be very different. The member states are required by this article to decide the criteria that will determine whether EIA will be necessary for projects in Annex II.

Article 5

Where a project is to be subjected to EIA, the information that must be provided in the report of the EIA should be based on the requirement given in Annex III. It is not, however, mandatory to include all of this information. Part 2 of this article gives the information that has to be included at all times, i.e. does not give discretion to the member state.

Member states are also given discretion as to whether they should insist that the authorities that receive the EIS make all the information they have available to the developer.

Article 6

This article is concerned with participation in the environmental assessment process.

Firstly, member states should make sure that any official bodies that have an interest in the project are given the opportunity to comment.

Secondly, members of the public should have the right to see the project application and the EIS, and should be allowed to comment before the project starts. Note that it is not before consent is given! Remarkably, it would be within the terms of this directive to grant consent before giving the public an opportunity to comment on the project.

Thirdly, minimum arrangements are given for the level and type of the public consultation.

Article 7

This concerns situations where activities in one member state may have significant effects in another, and requires that the EIS information be passed over to the other country at the same time as the public is informed in the country of the project's origin.

Article 8

This is a very short article but is crucial. This requires that the EIS has to be considered when the planning application is considered. Without this article, an EIS might be produced but would not have to be read!

Article 9

There is a duty of notification after the authority that has been delegated responsibility has reached a decision on the project. Although the decision has to be made public, whether the reasons behind it are also made public is left to the discretion of the member states.

Article 10

This article provides for non-release of information on two counts:

- commercial secrecy to prevent unfair competition; and

- public interest, for example defence projects.

Article 11

This is concerned with the pooling of information, monitoring and reporting back to the European Commission. There is a duty placed on the member states to submit information to the Commission. This is a common part of directives as member states will obviously implement directives differently. Thus, the next stage will be to harmonise practice across Europe at a future date. This article builds in a mechanism for modification of the directive after five years.

The wording of this article is interesting as it applies to the selection of projects in accordance with Article 4(2), i.e. Annex II. There is no specific provision for reporting back on experience gained in implementing Annex I, presumably because it is already well set out with thresholds.

Article 12

This is concerned with the implementation period for the directive. Each member state has to implement the directive within three years of its notification. Reference to the notification date at the bottom of the page shows that this was to occur by 3 July 1988.

Each member state is also obliged to explain how they have complied with the directive.

Article 13

The directive sets out minimum standards that must be met. These in no way prevent the member states from adopting more rigorous controls.

Article 14

This addresses the directive to the member states.

4.1.3   Annexes

The first two annexes guide the member states in screening. The third annex indicates what should be contained in an environmental statement. The following discussion of the individual annexes will look at these in more detail and indicate the actual obligations imposed and the parts that are merely advisory.

Annex I

This is very clear cut. There are nine project types, each of which has associated thresholds over which an environmental assessment must be carried out. There is no leeway for a member state to interpret these other than to introduce more stringent thresholds if they wish.

Annex II

This contains eleven separate classes of development: agriculture; extractive industry; energy industry; processing of metals; manufacture of glass; chemical industry; food industry; textile, leather, wood and paper industries; rubber industry; infrastructure projects; and finally, other projects.

Member states are obliged to use their discretion to decide which projects must always require environmental assessment, or to produce criteria indicating when an EIA is required. Reading Articles 2, 4 and then Annex II leads us to the conclusion that member states are not given scope to ignore Annex II projects; the scope is in determining what the criteria are for all of the projects. If categories were left out of a member state's national legislation, then this would be a breach of their obligation in implementing the directive.

Annex III

This annex provides advice on the information to include in an environmental statement. However, quite simply, it is the information in Article 5(2). Any information in Annex III additional to this is not something that each member state has to insist on being included in environmental statements. The additional information is left to the discretion of the member state as to whether they will require it.

The Environmental Assessment Directive is a simple document that is often a bit vague. For example, Article 12 specifies that member states must implement the directive by 3 July 1988, but does not say whether this will apply to projects for which planning application has been made but not yet approved, or for projects for which planning approval has yet to be sought by that date. This is an important point that did lead to disagreement between the European Commission and the government of the UK.

4.2   1993 and 1997 reviews of implementation

The European Commission published, in 1993, its review of the implementation of Directive 85/337/EEC. The 'five-year review' consists of a comparative analysis of implementation in all member states and separate, more detailed, country reports for each member state (Commission of the European Communities, 1993). In 1997, the review was updated (Commission of the European Communities, 1997). This section will detail what those reports said about EIA in the UK in particular, but will also refer to their comments on other countries to set the UK's position in its European context. The summary in this book is structured in such a way as to firstly investigate formal compliance with the directive, then to look at the practical application of the directive in the different member states, followed by an overall evaluation of Directive implementation. The 1993 report was summarised on Manchester University's EIA Centre web page (http://www.art.man.ac.uk/eia/EIAC.HTM), and the following summary of the 1993 and 1997 reports will follow the structure used there.

4.2.1 Main provisions of the directive

The 1993 report points out two key facts about the directive which have led to many of the conclusions. The first is that the nature of directives dictates that member states have a considerable amount of discretion in deciding how to meet the obligations they impose. The implications of this are that different approaches will be taken in different countries, and harmonisation of EIA laws will not be achieved. Secondly, the area of application of the directive is very broad and has an effect on a large number of different organisations in different sectors. As such, meeting the obligations imposed is no simple task as personnel within these many organisations have to change working practices or approaches.

Formal compliance

One feature of implementing directives is that some legally binding procedure has to be implemented in each member state, in other words new legislation. By July 1991 (the date at which research for the 1993 report ended), the research had shown that all countries had put in place some new legislation related to EIA. (Note that the European Community numbered only 12 countries in 1991 – Austria, Finland and Sweden had not then joined.) It is a feature of the complexity of implementing the legislation that some countries had to bring in many new regulations. In particular, the UK introduced 17 new regulations in the period July 1985 to July 1991, and Germany introduced 18. (As such the five-year review understated the actual number of regulations introduced in the UK as indicated in the next chapter.) The research did show, however, that many countries failed to meet their initial deadline of July 1988 for implementing these laws. While it was not the case in 1991 that the legislation in all countries fully complied with the directive, by the end of 1996 (the date at which research for the 1997 report ended), many countries had improved their legislation in the intervening period so that compliance was much better.

Annex I projects

Those projects listed under Annex I of the directive should, in theory, be easy to interpret for the member states and should lead to a good degree of harmonisation and compliance. This is because the requirements for EIA are quite clear and even have associated thresholds to indicate what constitutes a project likely to have significant effects on the environment and should therefore trigger an EIA. To some extent, the member states had fulfilled their obligations by July 1991, except for what the report calls 'partial exceptions'. These are clarified as:

> Belgium – nuclear-related activities; Germany – not in force for all Annex I projects until a Statutory Ordinance was adopted; Luxembourg – only Annex I road schemes were covered; Netherlands – some Annex I project categories were subject to a threshold exemption.

By the end of 1996, however, all countries had fully incorporated the Annex I requirements of the directive, barring Sweden which had yet to bring railways under EIA legislation.

Annex II projects

Annex II projects only need to undergo environmental assessment if member states decide that their impacts are significant enough. As such, the member states are afforded considerable discretion in deciding whether or not to perform EIA for projects listed in this annex. We would, therefore, expect some variability between different member states, and the 1993 report indicated that this was the case. The first example of variability was seen in the extent to which Annex II project categories and sub-categories were covered. The 1993 report indicated the coverage of these categories for all member states, but just three countries are presented here as examples – the UK because that is the focus of the book, Greece as an example of a member state with full compliance in this respect, and Spain with poor compliance (see Table 4.1). The Spanish case also indicates another problem which is also true of the UK, Belgium and Germany. That is, environmental legislation is not all centralised; there are separate regions with their own jurisdiction in this area, and these regions have to implement their own legislation in order to comply with the directive. Spain is divided into 17 regions, all of which need to implement their own EIA laws. Belgium has three regions, Germany has 16 Länder and the UK had, at the time, three regions as well in legal terms (England and Wales, Scotland and Northern Ireland).

Table 4.1 Annex II project coverage in selected member states

Member state	Coverage
Greece	All categories; all subcategories
Spain	At national level, no categories; some subcategories (1d, 2e, 2j, 10d, 10f, 10j); at regional level, some additional categories and subcategories
United Kingdom	All categories; most subcategories (all except 1a and 1b)

Full coverage means coverage of categories:

1   [agriculture] (subcategories a–h);

2   [extractive industry] (subcategories a–m);

3   [energy industry] (subcategories a–j);

4   [processing of metals] (subcategories a–k);

5   [manufacture of glass] (no subcategories);

6   [chemical industry] (subcategories a–c);

7   [food industry] (subcategories a–i);

8   [textile, leather, wood and paper industries] (subcategories a–f);

9   [rubber industry] (no subcategories);

10   [infrastructure projects] (subcategories a–j);

11   [other projects] (subcategories a–j);

12   [modifications to Annex I projects].

The second example of variability related to the threshold levels for projects applied within the same subcategories. One example of the large variability relates to pig-rearing installations. Typically, an installation for just 20 pigs would require an EIA in the Netherlands, but the installation would normally have to house 1,000 pigs in Ireland or 5,000 pigs in the UK before an EIA could be expected to be carried out. The 1997 report found that thresholds still varied widely, as did requirements for deciding whether EIA was necessary or not. It seemed that member states had not harmonised a great deal in regard to Annex II projects between 1991 and 1996.

Other areas of concern

The research for the 1993 report indicated a number of other areas of concern in relation to directive compliance. The issues raised were that the regulations implemented in some member states did not require all the information specified in the directive to be supplied in an environmental statement, that the obligations imposed for public consultation were not sufficient in all member states; and that there was no clear legal mechanism for forcing decision-makers to take account of the environmental statements in their decisions.

Additional provisions

While the five-year review highlights many deficiencies regarding implementation of the directive, it also identifies provisions where some member states have chosen to go further than the obligations imposed on them. Such provisions will lead to a lack of harmonisation across the European Union and therefore need some consideration.

Such provisions include extending the number of types of project listed in Annexes I and II of the directive and also extending the application of EIA to plans and programmes. Some countries have made formal provisions for scoping and, in the same vein, some countries require the consideration of alternatives. Other provisions made include requirements for checking the quality of EISs and requiring some form of monitoring of impacts to take place.

The research report does make it clear that since the research ended in July 1991, most member states made further changes to their EIA legislation and the number of deficiencies identified were reduced.

Practical application

It is interesting to look at the numbers of environmental statements produced in different member states, and at the types of project these were written for. Different legislation does lead to different numbers of environmental statements being produced, but the different cultures and industries typical of each member state also affects this. The research did look into this interesting area and produced Table 4.2.

Table 4.2 Estimates of the annual number of EISs prepared in each member state

Member state	Estimated annual average, 1988–90 approx.	Estimated annual forecast, post-1992	Estimated annual average in 1996
Austria			50 to 70
Belgium	43	125	95 to 105[3]
Denmark	6	15–40[1]	100
Finland			20 to 40
France	5,000	5,000	6,000
Germany	Not available	3,000	200 to 500
Greece	Not available	90–2,500[2]	1,200
Ireland	49	80	80
Italy	28	30–1,000[1]	200
Luxembourg	10	110[2]	10 to 20
Netherlands	67	140	100 to 120
Portugal	12	80	100
Spain	143	1,200	30 to 40[4]
Sweden			No data
United Kingdom	189	325	300 to 350

1   Larger estimate assumes extension of legislation to additional Annex II category projects.

2   Includes considerable numbers of 'mini' EISs.

3   Includes Flanders and Brussels only.

4   For large infrastructure projects – another 400 to 600.

Sources: Commission of the European Communities (1993); Lee and Jones (1993); Commission of the European Communities (1997).

So it is clear that there is a great variation in the number of environmental statements produced across the member states. In addition, it is also clear that the number being produced was increasing over time.

Quality of EISs

The review carried out for the research had no consistent approach to apply to the review of environmental statements. Instead, there was considerable reliance on the views of experts. Such views do give a good indication of the quality of the statements being produced at that time, though we have to remember that direct comparisons between member states are perhaps unreliable.

The findings were that some EISs were of good quality, but these were very much in the minority and most statements were very poor. This research is out of date now and the situation is thought to be improving. If we take the UK case in particular, more recent research by the EIA Centre based at Manchester University has shown that quality has continued to improve up to 1992, dramatically so between 1990 and 1992 in particular, with a slight decline in quality from 1992 up to March 1993 (Jones, 1995).

The 1997 report had little to add on the subject of quality as few additional studies had been carried out in the period since the 1993 report was written. The point was made that the directive is largely procedural and there was little the Commission could do to influence the quality of the final product.

Other areas of concern

The 1993 review found considerable variability in EIA practice, both between and within member states. In particular, scoping practices were identified as being extremely variable, as were practices for checking the quality of EISs. Together these two variations mean that EISs for similar projects are likely to be submitted with different contents in different member states, and the check performed by the authorities will be better in some countries.

In addition, the 1993 review identified a range of problems with public consultation and consultation in general. It was found that member states had limited availability of EISs for consultation, the consultation of authorities and the public was inadequately controlled, developments having potential transboundary impacts often did not require consultation with neighbouring countries, and the EIS itself and public comments did not always play a full role in the decision-making process (see Barker and Wood, 1999). The 1997 report did indicate that improvements had taken place in some countries in relation to consultation and participation, particularly in the Netherlands, Finland and Portugal.

4.3   Directive 97/11/EC

Reference to Article 11 of the 1985 Environmental Assessment Directive indicates that environmental assessment within the European Community is a process that will evolve. According to this article, we could have expected to have seen amendments as long ago as 1990 (five years after the notification of the directive). This process has, however, run late.

The initial step in formulating amendments to the directive was for the Commission to produce a five-year review of the implementation of the directive, the results of which were discussed in the previous section.

Following on from the five-year review, a proposal for an amended directive was released in May 1994 (Commission of the European Communities, 1994b), but was not adopted in its published form. Instead, in December 1995, the member states agreed a common position on an amended Directive. After completing the rest of the cooperation procedure, this Directive was adopted with only minor changes to its wording.

The full title is: 'Council Directive 97/11/EC of 3 March 1997 Amending Directive 85/337/EEC on the Assessment of the Effects of Certain Public and Private Projects on the Environment'.

The form of the directive is similar to the 1985 version; it has

- a preamble;

- articles;

- annexes.

4.3.1   Preamble

This is the first part of the directive, preceding the articles.

All the preamble does is set the background for the directive. We should, after reading the previous section, be aware that the original proposal for the directive would have come from the European

Commission, and that opinions would have been given on the proposal by both the European Parliament and the Economic and Social Committee. The preamble states this, and that the directive is a measure in line with the European Union action programmes on the environment and with the precautionary principle.

It is also stated that the directive is based on Article 130s.

In common with the 1985 directive, the main principles involved in environmental assessment are outlined:

- environmental assessment should be introduced for private and public projects likely to have significant effects on the environment;

- development consent will require possession of the environmental assessment information where it is appropriate to carry it out;

- there are separate categories of projects: those which will always require environmental assessment and those for which environmental assessment will only be required at the discretion of the member state;

- environmental assessment is necessary to take account of human health, to lead to a better environment and to ensure species diversity.

It also refers to the 1993 report on the implementation of the directive (Commission of the European Communities, 1993) to indicate the need for this amendment.

4.3.2   Articles

There are only five of these. The first article is the one that amends the text of Directive 85/337/EEC. It can look a little confusing because it refers to the articles of the previous directive in order to change them – it is easy to get lost and wonder whether you are looking at an article of Directive 97/11 or one of Directive 85/337.

To try and simplify things, this section will briefly look at what the articles in 97/11 say and then will go on to examine what the amended text of 85/337 now says. This is because the new directive (97/11/EC) changes the text of the old directive (85/337/EEC) – it does not simply revoke it. An informal consolidation (that is the directive as amended) is provided in Appendix 1 of this book.

Article 1 (97/11)

This amends the articles of the previous Environmental Assessment Directive. The specific changes will be outlined below.

Article 2 (97/11)

As in the previous directive, provision is made for a report to be sent to the European Parliament and Council on how well the amended directive has worked. As a result of this report, the next amendment will be prepared. In practice, the European Commission will tender for the report to be written, and the successful consultants will research and write the report.

Article 3 (97/11)

The deadline for meeting the obligations imposed by the amended directive is 14 March 1999. There is also an explicit statement pointing out exactly which projects will be covered by the directive on that date – those for which a request for development consent has been submitted. This text has been inserted because of all the problems caused by member states not knowing whether the directive applied to projects for which an application had not been made, or those for which the decision on the application had not yet made but the application had.

Article 4 (97/11)

This simply states that the directive comes into force on the twentieth day after its publication in the *Official Journal* (on 14 March 1997). This effectively means that the directive 85/337/EEC has duly been amended. It still only requires implementation by 14 March 1999, however.

Article 5 (97/11)

This addresses the directive to the member states.

The following articles refer to those of Directive 85/337/EEC as they have been amended by Article 1 of Directive 97/11/EC. It may prove useful to refer to Figure 4.2 while reading through this explanation – this is a flow chart of the new EIA process under the amended directive.

Article 1 (85/337 as amended)

No change to the original.

Article 2 (85/337 as amended)

A slight change has been made because of a loophole in the previous directive that allowed member states (like the UK) to exempt some projects from EIA requirements. Directive 85/337/EEC required environmental effects to be assessed for certain projects before development consent was given, the issue being that if a project listed in the directive was not subject to development consent, then this wouldn't happen! The UK government had plugged this loophole before this directive was amended.

There has been a feeling among workers in the environmental assessment field that separate procedures within member states on integrated pollution prevention and control duplicate some of the work required for environmental assessment. This is clearly inefficient and the directive allows a single procedure to be developed within the member states that covers both EIA and Integrated Pollution Prevention and Control (IPPC).

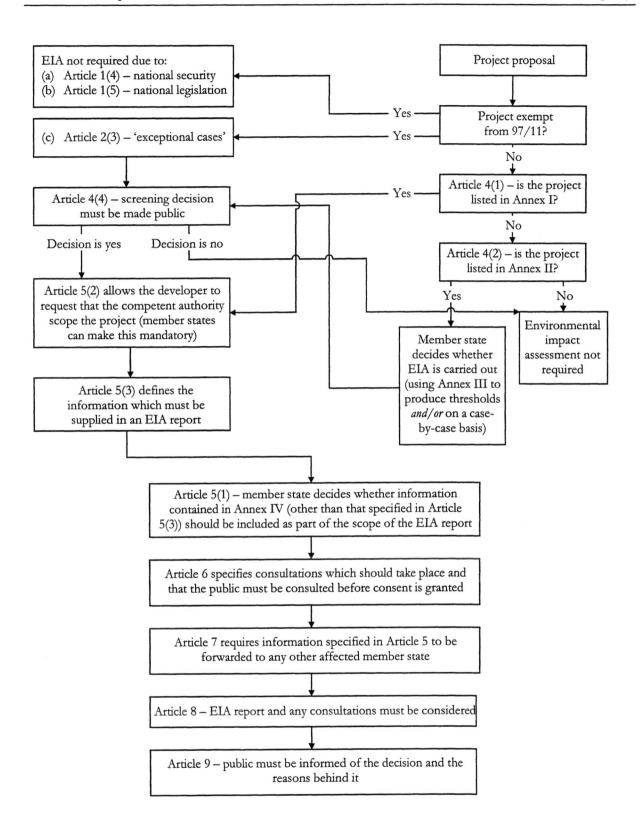

Figure 4.2 Flow chart showing the EIA obligations imposed on member states by the amended Environmental Assessment Directive (97/11/EC).

Article 3 (85/337 as amended)

This article spells out the types of environmental effects which should be investigated. The slight change here alters the order of the list of factors so that interactions of effects now also cover material assets and cultural heritage:

- human beings, fauna and flora;
- soil, water, air, climate and the landscape;
- material assets and the cultural heritage;
- the interaction between the factors mentioned in the first, second and third indents.

Article 4 (85/337 as amended)

This article still requires mandatory assessments of projects listed in Annex I (this annex is now longer – many projects have moved from the old Annex II to the new Annex I), and discretionary assessments of projects listed in Annex II (this annex has also changed as a result of new additions and the loss of some project types to Annex I). Member states are given discretion to apply specific thresholds for projects in Annex II, or to judge each project on a case-by-case basis, or to use a combination of the two. This formalises approaches that were already in use throughout Europe as a result of the original directive. At the same time, it does try to achieve more uniformity throughout – by indicating, in Annex III, the selection criteria which should be used both for setting thresholds and for decisions based on case-by-case approaches. (Note that this annex is now completely different from the same annex in the original directive). The screening decision made has to be made public – this is a welcome new addition.

Article 5 (85/337 as amended)

The contents of an environmental impact statement are now specified in Annex IV although, as with the previous version of the directive, this is not all mandatory. The mandatory component is set out in Article 5(3).

It is an important change that developers must now be given an opportunity to request that the competent authority set the scope for the environmental assessment (although this does not prevent the authority from requesting more information after the EIS has been submitted). Before the competent authority does this, it must consult the developer and the other authorities that are likely to be concerned by the project. Member states are given the right to insist that the competent authorities always scope the environmental assessment rather than only when asked by the developers.

Another important change is that Article 5(3) makes it compulsory for alternatives studied by the developer to be outlined in the EIS along with reasons for choosing a particular alternative ahead of the others.

Article 6 (85/337 as amended)

This requires member states to designate the authorities that must be consulted on the scope of the assessment and on the application itself at a later date. It is also made clear that the environmental statements must be sent to all the designated authorities.

The public must also have access to the environmental statement – the change here is that this must happen before the development consent is granted!

Article 7 (85/337 as amended)

This sets out much more precise requirements in the event of transboundary impacts and reflects the implementation of the Espoo Convention (UNECE, 1991) which deals with transboundary impacts and was signed by the European Union in 1991. It allows for the participation in the environmental assessment process of the country to be affected and its inhabitants.

Article 8 (85/337 as amended)

The addition to this requirement is that, as well as the environmental statement itself having to be considered as part of the consent procedure for the project concerned, so do the results of any consultations which have taken place.

Article 9 (85/337 as amended)

Once a decision on the development consent has been reached, the member states now have to inform the public of the reasons for reaching the decision as well as the actual decision itself. It is also a requirement that the public be informed of the mitigation measures, though it is not clear whether these are the measures specified in the EIS, or those which are part of the development approval process.

Where transboundary impacts occur, the affected member states must be supplied with the same information.

Article 10 (85/337 as amended)

This hasn't changed to any great degree. It has been reworded to make the meaning more precise (see Article 10 of 85/337/EEC on p. 82).

Article 11 (85/337 as amended)

It is specified that member states must inform the European Commission of any criteria or thresholds they adopt in their screening procedures. The rest of Article 11 remains unchanged.

Article 12 (85/337 as amended)

This is unchanged in so far as member states are required to report to the Commission details of measures taken to comply (see Article 12 of 97/11/EC on p. 82). This article also gave three years for compliance in Directive 85/337/EEC, but this requirement was superseded by the exact date of 14 March 1999 provided in Article 3 of 97/11/EC.

Article 13 (85/337 as amended)

This has been deleted! All it did was indicate that member states have the right to produce regulations that go further than the directive if they wish. However, this is a right that exists anyway, irrespective of its appearance in an article – for that reason the article was superfluous. You will see that this right exists from reading paragraph number 3 in the preamble (see Appendix 1).

Article 14 (85/337 as amended)

This is superseded by Article 5 of 97/11/EC.

4.3.3   Annexes

The first two annexes guide the member states in screening. The third annex indicates selection criteria that should be used in determining whether projects will have significant impacts with regard to Annex II projects. The fourth Annex indicates the contents of an environmental statement, but should be read in conjunction with Article 5(3). The Annexes are reproduced in Appendix 1.

Annex I

This is very clear-cut. There are 21 project types, each of which have associated thresholds over which an environmental assessment must be carried out. There is no leeway for a member state to interpret these other than to introduce more stringent thresholds if they wish.

Annex II

This contains 12 separate classes of development: agriculture, silviculture and aquaculture; extractive industry; energy industry; production and processing of metals; mineral industry; chemical industry; food industry; textile, leather, wood and paper industries; rubber industry; infrastructure projects;

other projects; tourism and leisure projects; and finally a section indicating that changes to existing developments falling under Annex I or II should be screened under Annex II.

Member states are obliged to use their discretion to decide which projects must always require environmental assessment subject to thresholds, or to produce criteria indicating when an EIA is required for them on a case-by-case basis.

Annex III

This lists the selection criteria (referred to in Article 4(3)) which must be used either to set thresholds or to make a screening decision on a case-by-case basis.

Annex IV

This sets out the information that ideally should be included in an environment statement. Note that there is no obligation on member states to require that all of the information specified in this annex appear in an EIS. The minimum information requirements are set out in Article 5(3).

4.4 Summary of changes made to Directive 85/337/EEC

Of interest to readers already familiar with Directive 85/337/EEC might be a quick summary of the main changes imposed on the EIA system across Europe by Directive 97/11/EC. These changes are outlined below using the same headings that were used to describe the EIA process in section 1.3. Remember this summarises extras, not the main provisions of the directive.

Public participation

*   Consultation has to take place with the public and environmental authorities in neighbouring member states likely to be affected by the development.

- Results of consultations have to be taken into account in the decision-making process.

- The reasons for making the decision have to be made public.

Screening

- There are 14 new categories of project for which EIA is mandatory (in Annex I), and some of the categories already subject to mandatory EIA have been extended.

- Modifications to projects falling within Annex II (those for which a system for making a decision on the need for EIA is made at the discretion of the member states) are themselves an Annex II category.

- There are more Annex II project types listed (or clarified): deforestation, marine and fluvial dredging of minerals, windfarms, asbestos production and manufacture of asbestos products, manufacture of ceramic products by burning, coastal works to combat erosion, groundwater abstraction and artificial groundwater recharge schemes, works for the transfer of water between river basins, ski runs, permanent camp sites and caravan sites, theme parks.

- There is a new Annex III which gives guidance on the selection criteria to be used for Annex II projects.

- Member states can either specify Annex II thresholds, or they can consider each project on a case-by-case basis, or they can use a combination of approaches.

- The reasoning behind the screening decision must be made public.

- Projects which are likely to have significant impacts on the environment have to be made subject to development consent. (This closes a loophole whereby projects would avoid the need for EIA in some cases because they didn't need a consent permit which would consider an EIS.)

Scoping

If the developer requests, the competent authority has to give their opinion on what information an EIS should contain. (Member states are allowed to make a scoping opinion from the competent authority compulsory in each case if they wish.)

Baseline study

As with the 1985 directive, no advice is given on this topic.

Impact prediction

The directive does not provide advice on such issues.

Impact assessment

The directive does not provide advice on such issues.

Mitigation

As part of the decision-making process, the mitigation measures adopted must be made public.

The environmental impact statement

The EIS has to consider alternatives studied by the developer.

EIS review

There are no review provisions – as with the 1985 directive.

Monitoring

There are no specific requirements to monitor developments to check on impacts.

As with the 1985 directive, there is a requirement for a five-year review of implementation.

Post-development audit

There are no post-development audit requirements.

CHAPTER 5

What Does UK EIA Legislation Specify?

This chapter will explain the UK EIA requirements as they currently stand. To do this, a short cut will have to be taken to allow for the separate arrangements which exist in Scotland, Northern Ireland and, since 1 July 1999, Wales for adopting delegated legislation. To explain what this means, in the UK laws are passed by the UK government in Westminster in the form of various Acts (such as the Town and Country Planning Act 1990). These Acts tend to state general principles to be followed rather than being specific about rules and regulations; instead, delegated legislation is used to enforce various parts of Acts of Parliament. To enforce the Environmental Assessment Directive, a large number of different regulations were needed to cover the different regional jurisdictions within the UK, and the different sectoral jurisdictions. The short cut mentioned will be to concentrate on the detail of just one regulation (as the others are similar in intent and form).

EIA legislation in the UK is a response to the amended European Council Directive 97/11/EC as discussed in the previous chapter. This chapter will go on to look at just what the law is in the UK, but first it is useful to consider how legislation in the UK has developed under the previous directive (85/337/EEC) for two reasons:

1. It will help the reader to understand screening decisions made in the past (environmental statements, for example, might indicate the regulations relevant to their production).

2. It will help the reader to understand why the legislation has developed in its current form because directives are not the only driving force.

5.1   Implementation of Directive 85/337/EEC

The simple solution to implementing a directive is to pass a single law which covers all the obligations of the directive. This was just not possible!

To give some background, the UK government has frequently been criticised for its limited implementation of Directive 85/337/EEC on Environmental Assessment which made no attempt to go further than the bare minimum allowed under the obligations imposed. Non-governmental organisations in particular were quite damning (for example, CPRE, 1992). Some of this criticism is justified on the basis that the initial protracted opposition of the UK government to the Environmental Assessment Directive is well documented (Wathern, 1988).

However, the legal situation in 1985 was that the UK government could not go further than the bare minimum allowed. This was because the European Communities Act 1972, the primary legislation which acceded to the precedence of what was then European Economic Community (EEC) legislation, allowed under section 2(2) for ministers to formulate and adopt secondary legislation to implement EEC legislation, but did not allow this legislation to go further than was required by directives (Wood, 1995). The reason for this does make perfect sense – the UK, as a signatory of the Treaty of Rome, was subject to legal obligations imposed from the EEC and had democratically agreed to this; however, as a democracy, it is unreasonable for the Secretary of State for the Environment to be able to implement regulations within the UK which go further than is required by an EEC directive without the agreement of Parliament. There was no primary legislation at that time which would, for example, allow the Secretary of State to extend the coverage of projects subject to EIA. It is, of course, open to debate whether the government should have passed primary legislation sooner.

Given this background of limited powers given to the Secretary of State for the Environment, why was it not possible to bring in just one regulation implementing all the obligations of the directive? The answer is simply because the focus of the directive is to integrate the requirement for EIA into decision-making processes. When the range of projects in the annexes to the directive are considered, they do not all fall within, for example, the decision-making processes associated with planning (i.e. the planning application process). It is true that most projects covered by the directive fall within the remit of planning where local authorities are the decision-makers (or the Secretary of State in some instance), but there are a number of groups of other projects falling outside the remit of planning, namely:

- afforestation;

- trunk roads and motorways which are approved under procedures set out in the Highways Act 1980;

- power stations, overhead power lines and long distance oil and gas pipelines – oil and gas pipelines which are over 10 miles in length fall within procedures set out in the Pipelines Act 1962 and power stations fall within procedures controlled by the Electricity Act 1989;

- land drainage improvements which are permitted developments under the General Development Order 1995;

- ports and harbours, which can undergo development outside the remit of the Town and Country Planning Act – depending on the nature of the work, this falls under either the remit of the Harbours Act 1964 or the Coast Protection Act 1949;

- marine salmon farming, which, if situated offshore, does not require planning permission – instead, a lease from the Crown Estate Commissioners is required;

- marine dredging for minerals – again, as the development is offshore, planning permission is not required and in this case a dredging licence has to be obtained from the Crown Estate Commissioners;

- offshore oil and gas production.

So, at the time the original EIA directive had to be implemented in July 1988, as well as projects covered within the remit of planning, separate regulations were needed to cover each of these areas. Added to this was the fact that separate regulations needed to be drawn up for England and Wales (the same regulations applied in both countries prior to the Welsh Assembly), Scotland and Northern Ireland! The net result was that, by the time the Department of Environment issued its *Guide to the Procedures* in 1989 (Department of the Environment, 1989), 20 sets of statutory instruments had come into force.

5.1.1   Background to planning in the UK

Prior to 1947, the lack of a structured planning policy had severe implications for public health. Planning, among many other duties, has to look at the needs for clean, uncontaminated water, the lack of which led to epidemics of cholera in the nineteenth century. In 1841, the life expectancy in England and Wales was only 41 years of age. In Liverpool, it was only 26. In 1843, the figure in Manchester was only 24 years of age. By the 1880s, this had only risen by five years (Hall, 1992).

Planning has improved considerably since those times, and these days, public health is relatively assured and we find our concerns more frequently being directed towards the implications of development on the environment. This was first reflected in concerns for the loss of agricultural land (Hall, 1992). Through the industrial revolution and into the 1930s, local authorities had no rights to stop development that wasn't in the public interest. This led to urban sprawl and an incredible use of good agricultural land. In the mid-1930s, 60,000 hectares of agricultural land per year were being built on out of 37 million hectares in total (in England and Wales). Worse than this, some of the best land was being used. The spread of London to the west used up much of the best market gardening land in England, the rest of which was later taken up by Heathrow airport.

The UK now has a well-established background of land use planning whereby permission is required before any development is allowed to take place. This dates back to the Town and Country Planning Act 1947 which introduced the requirement for development consent before development could take place. As a result of this, all that prevents development going ahead which is in the public interest is a lack of sufficient, good quality information. This need has ultimately culminated in environmental impact assessment trying to improve the consideration of the environment by providing better information within the planning process. Many changes have taken place since 1947, though none quite so radical. The situation now is that development is controlled by the Town and Country Planning Act 1990 and the Planning and Compensation Act 1991 which amended it in some important areas. Very briefly, the important points about the current planning system will be discussed.

Current planning background

There is a hierarchy of planning which goes from a national level at the top, to a regional level with separate administrative arrangements for England, Wales, Scotland and Northern Ireland. The national and regional levels are where policies and guidance are issued which must be implemented at a lower level.

Within England and Wales, there are an additional two types of structure – a two-tier system with county councils which have district councils within them, and also unitary authorities which carry out all the planning functions. The counties draw up *structure plans* which zone development at a regional level. The district councils draw up local plans that should conform with the structure plans. Together, the structure and local plans constitute the development plan. As regards planning permission, for most types of development, this is a local matter with authority residing with the district authorities. For some developments, such as waste disposal and minerals planning, these are deemed county matters and the county council has authority. The unitary authorities preside over all planning matters.

In Scotland, regional councils have equivalent duties of the county councils in England and Wales, and there are nine of them with 53 district councils. In addition, there are three island authorities. The situation is further complicated because not all the local authorities in Scotland have planning powers!

Northern Ireland is different again and is run centrally, all from the Department of the Environment (Northern Ireland). All these differences in administrative structure complicate the implementation of the EU directive as we shall see.

It is important to stress that the planning system described here is that which has been created by the above two Acts, plus their equivalents in Scotland and Northern Ireland. The situation can easily change if other Acts of Parliament are passed. In general, then, development plans state the policies of the local authorities within their own areas. They identify needs for their areas and zone specific types of development to specific areas accordingly. It is a very important point that, since the Planning and Compensation Act 1991, the development plan is the most important consideration in dealing with an application for development consent. The following phrase is added to the Town and Country Planning Act 1990 as section 54A:

> Where, in making any determination under the planning Acts, regard is to be had to the development plan, the determination shall be made in accordance with the plan unless material considerations indicate otherwise.

What are the material considerations? A lot of case law has developed in defining these, the outcome of which seems to be that any consideration which relates to the development and use of land can be a material consideration. The most common considerations are, however, current government policy (in the form of planning policy guidance documents), the views of statutory consultees (bodies with expertise and authority in specific areas, for example the Environment Agency in relation to rivers and streams), the views of the public and environmental impact statements.

Thus, the practical use of EIA can be seen within the planning system. Another consideration which we need to be aware of is the scope of planning. We know from our discussion of the Environmental Assessment Directive, which projects need to be covered by a member state's legislation. If all of these projects fall within the scope of the Town and Country Planning Act 1990, then implementation of the directive is an easy matter since development consent can simply be withheld in the absence of an EIS where one is required. However, if project types specified in the annexes of the directive do not fall within this Act, then the situation becomes much more complicated.

Development is defined in section 55(1) of the Town and Country Planning Act 1990 as: 'the carrying out of building, engineering, mining or other operations in, on, over or under land' or 'the making of any material change in the use of any land'. The terms 'building', 'engineering' and 'mining' are all defined (but 'other operations' is not). Thus, there are two meanings for development. The first is what we traditionally understand as development; the second is a change in the use to which land is put. We will not go any further into material change of use as, although important for planning purposes, this type of development does not require EIA.

For EIA, we are also particularly interested in the contents of section 58 of the Town and Country Planning Act 1990. This requires the Secretary of State to make an order, known simply as the General Development Order (GDO), providing for the granting of planning permission. Such an order grants automatic planning permission for certain developments that it specifies. The Secretary of State made the Town and Country Planning (General Permitted Development) Order 1995 (SI 1995 No. 418). The Order divides the project types into 33 parts, for which planning permission from the local authority or the Secretary of State is not required (more accurately, it is deemed to be granted). Table 5.1 lists these parts.

Many of these parts of the GDO only permit maintenance work of various kinds, for example part 16. Two of the classes, however, have the potential to exempt projects that are large enough to warrant consideration for an EIA from the requirement for planning permission. These are parts 6 and 7 concerning agriculture and forestry.

Table 5.1 Permitted development under the GDO (1995)

Part	Project type
1	Development within the curtilage of a dwelling house
2	Minor operations
3	Changes of use
4	Temporary buildings and uses
5	Caravan sites
6	Agricultural buildings and operations
7	Forestry buildings and operations
8	Industrial and warehouse development
9	Repairs to unadopted streets and private ways
10	Repairs to services
11	Development under local or private Acts or orders
12	Development by local authorities
13	Development by local highway authorities
14	Development by drainage authorities
15	Development by [The Environment Agency]
16	Development by or on behalf of sewerage undertakers
17	Development by statutory undertakers
18	Aviation development
19	Development ancillary to mining operations
20	Coal mining development by the coal authority and licensed operators
21	Waste tipping at a mine
22	Mineral exploitation
23	Removal of material from mineral-working deposits
24	Development by telecommunications code system operators
25	Other telecommunications development
26	Development of the Historic Building and Monuments Commission for England
27	Use by members of certain recreational organisations
28	Development at amusement parks
29	Driver information systems
30	Toll road facilities
31	Demolition of buildings
32	Schools, colleges, universities and hospitals
33	Closed circuit television cameras

Considering part 6 first, class A of this part permits the carrying out on agricultural land, comprised in an agricultural unit, of:

(a)   works for the erection, extension or alteration of a building; or

(b)   any excavation or engineering operations, which are reasonably necessary for the purposes of agriculture within that unit.

Although this is hedged around with stipulations as to the circumstances where this exemption is applicable, the basic position is that agricultural building or other operations do not require planning permission because (in most cases) it is a permitted development.

In relation to forestry, part 7, class A permits

the carrying out on land used for the purposes of forestry, including afforestation, of development reasonably necessary for those purposes consisting of –

(a)   works for the erection, extension or alteration of a building;

(b)   the formation, alteration or maintenance of private ways;

(c)   operations on that land, or on land held or occupied with that land, to obtain the materials required for the formation, alteration or maintenance of such ways,

(d)   other operations (not including engineering or mining operations).

So we can see that there is the potential for some projects to bypass the planning process and, therefore, the need for EIA. We will come back to this issue later.

5.1.2   Development of EIA regulations within the remit of planning

The Town and Country Planning (Assessment of Environmental Effects) Regulations 1988 (SI 1199) covered the vast majority of all projects requiring EIA in the UK. Research by Oxford Brookes University (Bellanger and Frost, 1997) showed that, up to January 1997, 91% of EISs submitted in the UK were required by this particular Statutory Instrument.

Table 5.2 lists the UK EIA regulations in place up to the time when the amended directive (97/11/EC) had to be implemented. It will be useful to refer to this as you read through the following sections.

Table 5.2 EIA regulations adopted in the UK prior to obligations under the amended Directive 97/11/EC being met

Planning – England & Wales

Town and Country Planning (Assessment of Environmental Effects) Regulations 1988 (Statutory Instrument No. 1199)

Town and Country Planning (Assessment of Environmental Effects) (Amendment) Regulations 1990 (Statutory Instrument No. 367)

Town and Country Planning (Assessment of Environmental Effects) (Amendment) Regulations 1992 (Statutory Instrument No. 1494)

Town and Country Planning (Assessment of Environmental Effects) (Amendment) Regulations 1994 (Statutory Instrument No. 677)

Town and Country Planning General Development (Amendment) Order 1994 (Statutory Instrument No. 678)

Town and Country Planning (Environmental Assessment and Permitted Development) Regulations 1995 (Statutory Instrument No. 417)

Town and Country Planning (General Permitted Development) Order 1995 (Statutory Instrument No. 418) [Article 3 introduces EA for otherwise Permitted Development]

Town and Country Planning (General Development Procedure) Order 1995 (Statutory Instrument No. 419)

Town and Country Planning (Simplified Planning Zones) Regulations 1992 (Statutory Instrument No. 2414) (Regulation 22 refers to EA)

Town and Country Planning (Environmental Assessment and Unauthorised Development) Regulations 1995 (Statutory Instrument No. 2258)

Planning – Scotland

Town and Country Planning (General Development) (Scotland) Amendment Order 1988 (Statutory Instrument No. 977)

Environmental Assessment (Scotland) Regulations 1988 (Statutory Instrument No. 1221)

Town and Country Planning (General Development Procedure) (Scotland) Order 1992 (Statutory Instrument No. 224) (Article 16)

Environmental Assessment (Scotland) Amendment Regulations 1994 (Statutory Instrument No. 2012 S.91)

Town and Country Planning, The Environmental Assessment (Scotland) Amendment Regulations 1997 (Statutory Instrument No. 1870 S.136)

Town and Country Planning (General Permitted Development) (Scotland) Amendment Order 1997 (Statutory Instrument No. 1871 S.137)

Table 5.2 (contd)

Planning – Northern Ireland

Planning (Assessment of Environmental Effects) Regulations (Northern Ireland) 1989 (Statutory Rule No. 20)

Environmental Assessment (Afforestation) Regulations (Northern Ireland) 1989 (Statutory Rule No. 226)

Drainage (Environmental Assessment) Regulations (Northern Ireland) 1991 (Statutory Rule No. 376)

Roads (Northern Ireland) Order 1993 (Statutory Rule No. 3160 NI 15) (Article 67)

Roads (Assessment of Environmental Effects) Regulations (Northern Ireland) 1994 (Statutory Rule No. 316).

Planning (Simplified Planning Zones) (Excluded Development) Order (Northern Ireland) 1994 (Statutory Rule 1994 No. 426)

Planning (Assessment of Environmental Effects) (Amendment) Regulations (Northern Ireland) 1994 (Statutory Rule No. 395)

Planning (General Development) (Amendment) Order (Northern Ireland) 1995 (Statutory Rule No. 356)

Planning (Environmental Assessment and Permitted Development) Regulations (Northern Ireland) 1995 (Statutory Rule No. 357)

Afforestation

Environmental Assessment (Afforestation) Regulations 1988 (Statutory Instrument No. 1207)

Environmental Assessment (Afforestation) Regulations (Northern Ireland) 1988 (Statutory Rule No. 226)

Land drainage improvements

Land Drainage Improvement Works (Assessment of Environmental Effects) Regulations 1988 (Statutory Instrument No. 1217)

Land Drainage Improvement Works (Assessment of Environmental Effects) (Amendment) Regulations 1995 (Statutory Instrument No. 2195)

Part V (Drainage Works) of the Environmental Assessment (Scotland) Regulations 1988 (Statutory Instrument No. 1221)

Drainage (Environmental Assessment) Regulations (Northern Ireland) 1991 (Statutory Rule No. 376)

Marine salmon farming

Environmental Assessment (Salmon Farming in Marine Waters) Regulations 1988 (Statutory Instrument No. 1218)

Trunk roads and motorways

Highways (Assessment of Environmental Effects) Regulations 1988 (Statutory Instrument No. 1241)

Table 5.2 (contd)

Highways (Assessment of Environmental Effects) Regulations 1994 (Statutory Instrument
No. 1002)

Part VI (Amendments of the Roads (Scotland) Act 1984) of the Environmental Assessment
(Scotland) Regulations 1988 (Statutory Instrument No. 1221)

Roads (Assessment of Environmental Effects) Regulations (Northern Ireland) 1994 (Statutory Rule
No. 316)

Railways, tramways, inalnd waterways and works interfering with navigation rights

Transport and Works (Application and Objections Procedure) Rules 1992 (Statutory Instrument
No. 2902)

Transport and Works (Assessment of Environmental Effects) Regulations 1995 (Statutory
Instrument No. 1541) (Amends Statutory Instrument 1992 No. 2902)

Ports and harbours

Harbour Works (Assessment of Environmental Effects) Regulations 1988 (Statutory Instrument
No. 1336)

Harbour Works (Assessment of Environmental Effects) (No. 2) Regulations 1989 (Statutory
Instrument No. 424)

Harbour Works (Assessment of Environmental Effects) Regulations 1992 (Statutory Instrument
No. 1421)

Harbour Works (Assessment of Environmental Effects) (Amendment) Regulations 1996 (Statutory
Instrument No. 1946)

Harbour Works (Assessment of Environmental Effects) Regulations (Northern Ireland) 1990
(Statutory Rule No. 181)

Power stations, overhead power lines and long-distance oil and gas pipelines

Electricity and Pipeline Works (Assessment of Environmental Effects) Regulations 1990 (Statutory
Instrument No. 442)

Electricity and Pipeline Works (Assessment of Environmental Effects) (Amendment) Regulations
1996 (Statutory Instrument No. 422)

Electricity and Pipeline Works (Assessment of Environmental Effects) (Amendment) Regulations
1997 (Statutory Instrument No. 629)

Part III (Electricity Applications) of the Environmental Assessment (Scotland) Regulations 1988
(Statutory Instrument No. 1121)

Projects approved by private Act of Parliament

Standing Order 27A. 20 May 1991

General Order 27A. 20 May 1992. Inserted by Private Legislation Procedure (Scotland) General
Order 1992 (Statutory Instrument No. 1992/1206)

The form of each of these regulations is broadly similar and, for ease of explanation, just the provisions of SI 1199 will be explained in detail. The justification for this is simply that only 9% of projects in the UK have been subject to EIA under all the other Regulations listed in Table 5.2.

The form of SI 1199 was very similar to that of the EU Directive (85/337/EEC). It had three schedules: Schedule 1 listed the projects for which EIA was mandatory, Schedule 2 listed projects for which EIA was carried out at the discretion of the local planning authority, and Schedule 3 listed the information which an environmental statement had to contain, and that which it should contain (much as Annex III of the directive). The process itself under SI 1199 is summarised in Figure 5.1.

The action-forcing section of SI 1199 was section 4(2) which stated:

> The local planning authority or the Secretary of State or an inspector shall not grant planning permission pursuant to an application to which this regulation applies unless they have first taken the environmental information into consideration.

At January 1997, the tally of environmental statements submitted in the UK stood at 2,776. The number produced annually peaked in 1991 at just fewer than 400 and has declined every year since (Bellanger and Frost, 1997). Kent has received the greatest number of EISs up to January 1997 (122). The most common categories requiring EISs are waste disposal projects (20%), roads (17%), mineral extraction (14%) and the energy sector (13%) of which 106 out of the 363 projects were windfarms.

A developer could either choose to carry out an EIA on a voluntary basis, or ask the local planning authority for a direction. In the latter case, the process to be followed is stipulated in section 5 of the regulations and is illustrated in Figure 5.2.

From the time the local authority receives the request for a direction, they have three weeks in which to decide whether an EIA is necessary. They can request more information from the developer if they feel they don't have enough to make a decision. The developer has the right to appeal against the decision (or the lack of a decision). In practice, this would only happen if they were requested to carry out an EIA because of the cost involved.

The Secretary of State for the Environment would then have three weeks in which to make a decision, and could again request more information if needed (section 6 of the regulations).

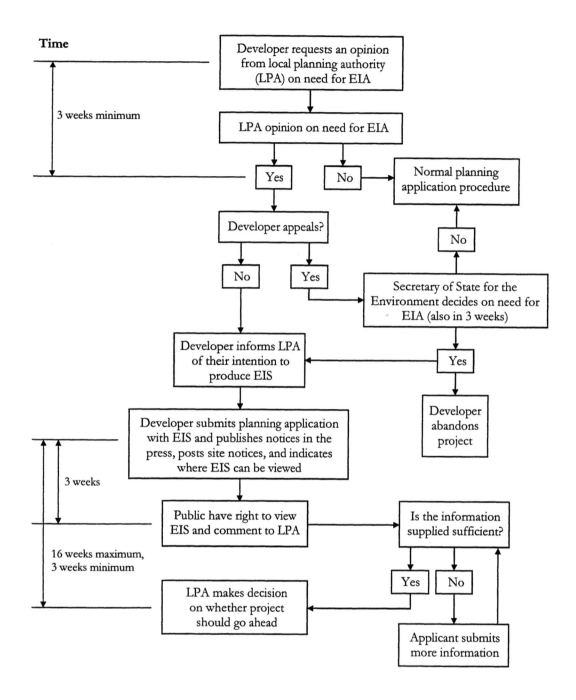

Figure 5.1 EIA procedure in the UK under SI 1199.

In practice, screening decisions in the early days were subject to errors because the local planning authorities had a poor understanding of the new regulations and how they really worked. The availability of training and generally increased awareness of EIA helped this situation which continued to improve. The UK government also published a guide to the procedures (Department of the Environment, 1989) which contained a section on indicative criteria for making screening decisions.

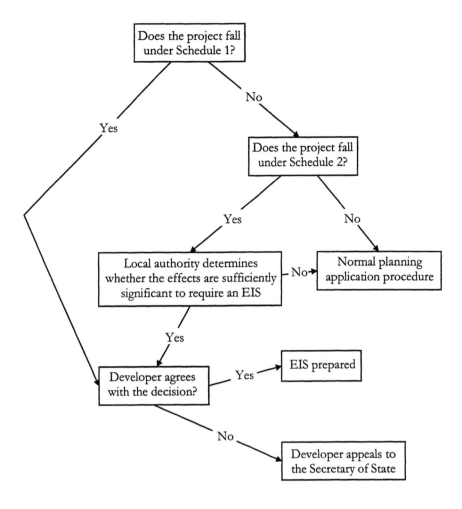

Figure 5.2 Procedure for screening where the local planning authority is asked for a direction.

These set out 'thresholds' that could be used as guidance as to what constitutes a significant impact and thus requires EIA. For example, for Schedule 2 projects: 'New pig rearing installations will not generally require EA: however, those designed to house more than 400 sows or 5,000 fattening pigs may require EA.' The guidance was useful; however, there was always a tendency when provided with such guidance to have it applied it too rigidly as the nature, size and location of the project were supposed to be determining factors in the UK. Such discretion almost certainly led to inconsistent decisions between different local authorities and is presumably a driving factor behind the changes to the UK regulations to be discussed later.

Scoping was not carried out under the regulations. Schedule 3 set out the information which had to be contained within an EIS, and also the information that should ideally have been in there but was not legally required. Thus, the developer identifies the aspects that will be covered in an EIS, subject to some minimum requirements.

The opportunities for public involvement were not great. The regulations made it clear that the public had to have access to the environmental statement, and they had to be informed of this fact by the developer who was obliged to publish an advert in a local newspaper telling them where they could see and obtain copies (sections 13 and 14 of the regulations).

Beyond this, the public had the right to comment on the EIS during the first 21 days after it had been submitted along with the planning application (some of the other regulations implementing the directive in the UK give up to 42 days). The local planning authority in reaching their decision should then have taken the comments into consideration. The regulations prevented the local authority, which had 16 weeks to make their decision, from taking less than 21 days to make it.

The UK legislation has no provision for the independent review of environmental statements nor for post-development monitoring of the project's environmental effects.

This book has previously referred to the fact that regulations like SI 1199 did no more than attempt minimum compliance with the directive. However, in 1991 the Planning and Compensation Act introduced section 71A into the Town and Country Planning Act 1990 which provides the Secretary of State for the Environment with the power to introduce regulations that go further than the requirements of the directive.

As we have seen, UK legislation follows the directive very closely: the annexes are mirrored by Schedules 1, 2 and 3 of SI 1199 (1988) for projects which fall under the remit of planning. The EIA procedures are triggered by the requirement for a planning application, which must, for developments which are deemed to require them, be accompanied by an environmental statement.

While the Environmental Assessment Directive (Commission of the European Communities, 1985) required implementation of legislation within all the member states of the European Community by 3 July 1988, in the UK, implementation was not complete by the required date for any project types at all.

Within the field of planning, the first amendments to legislation were made on 31 March 1990 with SI 367. This amendment came about as a result of the privatisation of the Central Electricity Generating Board (CEGB); previously, CEGB projects were approved by the Secretary of State for Energy, and nuclear power stations were covered by SI 167 (1989). After the demise of the CEGB, SI 167 was revoked by SI 442 (1990) and nuclear power stations were brought within the remit of planning by adding the category of nuclear power stations or other nuclear reactors to Schedule 1 (i.e. projects which always require EIA) of SI 1199 (1988).

Since that particular amendment, a number of loopholes in the EIA regulations were identified and closed using further amending regulations. The loopholes the various amendments address are, in chronological order, as follows;

- Planning authorities could bypass EA requirements where they were the developers.

- Permitted developments (those specified in the General Development Order as having automatic planning permission) bypass EIA requirements.

- Unauthorised developments, where a developer proceeds without having sought planning permission, can lead to the granting of planning permission without the need for EA via an enforcement notice appeal.

Further to these required changes, some improvements were made to the procedures going beyond the requirements of the directive:

- extra categories of project were introduced into Schedule 2.

These are discussed in more detail below.

Planning authorities as developers

SI 1494 (1992) closes the loophole whereby local authorities were not required to submit a planning application if they were the developers and, thus, bypassed EIA requirements. SI 1494 inserts an extra regulation into SI 1199 (1988) which specifically requires an environmental statement from local authorities in cases where environmental effects will be significant.

Permitted developments

SI 417 (1995) was introduced under powers conferred only by section 2(2) of the European Communities Act. This, in itself, indicates that all the changes are still within the obligations imposed on the UK by the Environmental Assessment Directive. This regulation needs to be considered together with the General Permitted Development Order (SI 418, 1995).

To summarise the problem addressed by SI 417 (1995), the General Permitted Development Order grants planning permission (permitted development) for some categories of project (some of which are required to be the subject of environmental assessment under the directive); in particular, many types of agricultural development are granted permission. To close the loophole, the government would have to require environmental assessment for projects which have significant effects but for which planning permission would have been automatically granted. The loophole was actually closed by the General Permitted Development Order in section 3(10) which says:

> …development is not permitted by this Order if an application for planning permission for that development would be a Schedule 1 application or a Schedule 2 application within the meaning of the Town and Country Planning (Assessment of Environmental Effects) Regulations 1988…
>
> SI No. 418, 1995

This put the onus on the planning authorities to determine where such developments are taking place and serve enforcement notices where necessary – no mean task for agricultural buildings of which planning authorities often have no knowledge of their construction.

Unauthorised developments

Bearing in mind that it is not a crime to develop without planning permission, but that it is a crime not to comply with the enforcement notice which may follow such an act (where material harm has been or would be caused), there was a possibility of a development being built without planning permission having been sought, and for planning permission to be granted by means of winning the appeal to the Secretary of State against the enforcement notice. This would bypass the need for environmental assessment which is associated with the planning application process.

Regulation 3 of SI 2258 prevents the Secretary of State from granting planning permission on the determination of an enforcement notice appeal without first considering an environmental statement if the project would have required environmental assessment under the EIA regulations.

Broadening the scope of EIA

SI 677 introduced in 1994 (under powers conferred by section 71A of the Town and Country Planning Act 1990) was a significant step forward in that the powers given to the Secretary of State to go further than is required by the directive were used to expand the range of projects covered by regulations in the UK. Three extra categories of project were added to Schedule 2 of the EIA regulations: wind generators, motorway service areas, coastal protection works. A significant omission from the list of new Schedule 2 projects was that of golf courses – this had been expected to be present as it had appeared in draft issues of the regulations, and it was one of the extra project categories in Annex II of the proposed amendment to the Environmental Assessment Directive (Commission of the European Communities, 1994b).

It is also interesting to note that the application of these amendments was specifically exempted from projects for which the planning application had already been submitted on the day it came into force. The other changes made by the amendment were: the introduction of specific procedures for publicity regarding further information that may be required by the local authority, and the requirement for submission of more copies of the environmental statements.

We can see, therefore, that progress was made to close the loopholes created where implemented regulations did not comply fully with Directive 85/337/EEC. Considering the large numbers of amendments introduced to achieve this, however, the question is inevitably raised as to how many loopholes remain?

5.1.3   Loopholes remaining in the UK under the 85/337/EEC implementing regulations

Further to compliance with Directive 85/337, several loopholes still remained (Bond, 1997). In brief, these were as follows:

- Sand mining can bypass requirements because of the peculiar characteristics associated with this type of development.

- Interim Development Orders granted before 1947 bypass EIA requirements.

- In terms of housing, new villages, unless they contain sufficient commercial development, were exempted by Department of Environment guidance.

These are discussed in turn below.

Sand mining

The mining of sand from beaches is a development with unusual characteristics. Unlike the extraction of ores from traditional mines or quarries, the resource is constantly replenished by the action of tides.

Where a planning application is made for mining, permission is given to mine a specific area detailed in the application. Should this area require extension in the future, such as is often the case with traditional quarries, a further planning application is required and the EIA regulations thus apply. The peculiar case of sand mining, however, arguably does not require a change in the area set out in the application but a change in the time span of the mining operation itself – something contained in the conditions accompanying the planning permission which can be varied without the need for a new planning application. Therefore it is possible, where an authority grants permission for the conditions to be varied, for EIA to be bypassed.

Interim Development Orders

Environmental assessment loopholes exist as a result of historical town and country planning legislation. Interim Development Orders (IDO) granted on or after 22 July 1943 and before 1 July 1948 are still in force today. Those granted before the 1947 Town and Country Planning Act were not even required to be registered and so the records of the estimated 1,000 of these were, until recently, sparse or non-existent.

The government went some way to remedying the lack of regulation of these sites by requiring, in the Planning and Compensation Act 1991, that holders of these permissions had to apply to the mineral planning authority for registration of the permission, followed by an application for determination of conditions. In England and Wales, registration was required by 25 March 1992 and 630 applications for registration were received up to that date (Anon., 1992).

The fact is that 630 applications for registration were made for developments which were not subjected to rigorous environmental appraisal, and which had, apparently, bypassed environmental assessment legislation. More will be said on this point in the later section on UK case law.

Housing

Directive 85/337/EEC has urban development as one of the categories under Annex II. The UK legislation has transferred this heading to section 10(b) of Schedule 2 to SI 1199. However, new housing schemes are not specifically mentioned and guidance (DoE, 1989) specifically states that:

> Such schemes (other than purely housing schemes) may require EA where...

Glasson et al. (1994) report that an early ruling by the DoE indicated that a proposal for 3,000 houses near Cambridge did not fall into Schedule 1 or 2 of SI 1199 and EIA was not, therefore, required.

Bearing in mind that the final arbiters of decisions to require EIA are the local planning authorities or the Secretary of State on appeal, the result of this guidance is either that new villages or extension to housing estates are not subject to the requirements of environmental assessment, or that developers have strong grounds for appeal where an EIS is requested. The potential outcome of not carrying out

EIA is that housing development may be allowed to proceed leading to a situation where the infrastructure for extra housing (roads, water supply, electricity supply, etc.) is already in place, thereby encouraging developers to apply for more housing developments. This situation would be an example of cumulative impacts arising.

5.2   Implementation of Directive 97/11/EC

The UK government had until 14 March 1999 to meet the obligations imposed on it by Directive 97/11/EC.

To meet these new obligations, the Department of Environment, Transport and the Regions undertook a consultation exercise on the new regulations. The first consultation paper was issued on 28 July 1997, followed by a second consultation paper on 19 December 1997, followed by draft regulations which were circulated on 16 July 1998. The main points of each of these consultation exercises will be set out in turn.

5.2.1   July 1997 consultation exercise

The July 1997 consultation exercise set out the requirements of the amended directive and the government's proposals. At this stage, the consultation document was not a draft set of regulations but simply a statement of current intent for comment by anyone who wished to do so. The consultation paper was very useful in identifying all the changes to the existing directive in separate appendices, thereby making it easier for readers with experience of that directive to comment on the government's proposals for change.

The consultation paper was also interesting because it set out, in its Appendix VII, a 'Synopsis of Compliance Cost Assessment Prepared in April 1995 and Updated in November 1995'. This gives a broad estimate of the cost of producing environmental statements in the UK, the additional costs likely to be incurred due to an anticipated increase in the number of EISs required and a likely increase in the cost of their production. In short, it is estimated that the average EIS will cost from £25,000 to £45,000, with a median cost of £35,000 being £5,000 higher than the median cost to produce an EIS under the regulations in place to comply with Directive 85/337/EEC. Using 1993 figures for annual EIS production of 350, and assuming an extra 15% per year as a result of the amended regulations under consultation, another 55 EISs were expected. So, considering an extra £5,000 for 350 EISs and an extra £25,000 to £45,000 for the extra 55 EISs, the cost to UK business was put at between £3,125,000 and £4,225,000 per year (DETR, 1997a).

Since the consultation document was released, a court case heard in the House of Lords in February 1999 has led to the expectation of up to 20 extra EISs per year being required for reviews of old minerals permissions. Each of these EISs is expected to cost from £13,000 to £25,000. If we assume a low end estimate of 10 per year at £13,000 and an upper end of 20 per year at £25,000, the figures in the above paragraph can be updated to read an extra cost to UK business of between £3,255,000 and £4,725,000. These estimates seem set to rise rather than fall if this trend continues!

5.2.2 December 1997 consultation exercise

Based on the responses to the July 1997 consultation exercise, the UK government decided to adopt a screening strategy for Annex II projects of the directive (that is, those for which EIA is at the discretion of the member state) based on the use of:

•   exclusive thresholds for most project categories, the idea being that if a project fell below given thresholds, then there would be no need for EIA;

•   case-by-case consideration – this continues the strategy adopted under Directive 85/337/EEC except that there would be improved guidance on what constitutes significant. This type of screening decision would only be made where a project did not fall below the exclusive threshold.

The consultation document presented a figure to explain the screening system being suggested which is reproduced in Figure 5.3. The document lists 'sensitive areas' which are areas of land with certain designations as listed in Table 5.3.

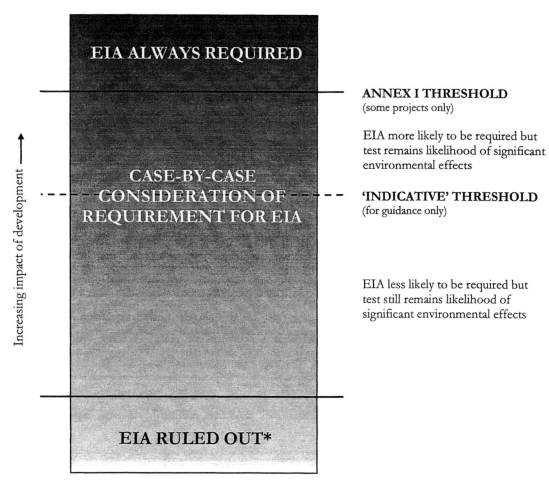

*Exceptionally, the Secretary of State (or the Department of the Environment in Northern Ireland) may direct that a project requires EIA even though it is below the 'exclusive' threshold and outside a 'sensitive area'.

Figure 5.3 The threshold system proposed to screen projects for EIA in the UK.

(*Source*: DETR, 1997b.)

The proposal for comment by those consulted was that exclusive thresholds should not apply for projects within these sensitive areas. Also for comment were a list of proposed exclusive thresholds and indicative thresholds for those projects which which were not excluded. This list of thresholds was almost certainly based on a DETR research contract awarded to Oxford Brookes University which had a remit to develop the indicative criteria in place for the existing EIA regulations.

Table 5.3 Sensitive areas as specified in DETR (1997b)

- Sites and Areas of Special Scientific Interest (SSSIs and ASSIs) including:
    - Ramsar Sites (sites designated for their importance as waterfowl habitat under the Ramsar Convention on Wetlands of International Importance)
    - Special Protection Areas (SPAs)
    - Special Areas of Conservation (SACs)
    - National Nature Reserves (NNRs)
- World Heritage Sites and Scheduled Ancient Monuments (SAMs)
- National Parks, The Broads and the New Forest Heritage Area
- Areas of Outstanding Natural Beauty (AONBs), National Scenic Areas (NSAs) and Natural Heritage Areas (NHAs)

5.2.3 July 1998 consultation exercise

By this stage, the government had produced draft regulations and these formed the basis of the consultation exercise. No major changes to these draft regulations were made to the regulations adopted in 1999 which will be considered below.

5.3 The 1999 EIA regulations

As with implementation of the 1985 Environmental Assessment Directive, a number of regulations should have been in place by the appointed date (14 March 1999 for Directive 97/11/EC) to meet all the imposed obligations. Table 5.4 illustrates the four regulations in place by the required date; reference back to Table 5.2 will demonstrate that there is still a long way to go for full compliance!

Table 5.5 indicates the additional regulations adopted to comply with the amended directive up to mid November 1999. It is clear that the UK government has failed to meet all its obligations.

Table 5.4 New regulations implementing Directive 97/11/EC in the UK
up to end March 1999

England and Wales

The Town and Country Planning (Environmental Impact Assessment)(England and Wales)
    Regulations 1999 (Statutory Instrument No. 293)

The Offshore Petroleum Production and Pipe-lines (Assessment of Environmental Effects)
    Regulations 1999 (Statutory Instrument No. 360)

The Environmental Impact Assessment (Fish Farming in Marine Waters) Regulations 1999
    (Statutory Instrument No. 367)

The Highways (Assessment of Environmental Effects) Regulations 1999 (Statutory Instrument
    No. 369)

Table 5.5 New regulations implementing Directive 97/11/EC in the UK
since end March 1999

The Public Gas Transporter Pipe-line Works (Environmental Impact Assessment) Regulations 1999
    (Statutory Instrument No. 1672)

The Environmental Impact Assessment (Land Drainage Improvement Works) Regulations 1999
    (Statutory Instrument No. 1783)

The Environmental Impact Assessment (Forestry) (England and Wales) Regulations 1999 (Statutory
    Instrument No. 2228)

Nuclear Reactors (Environmental Impact Assessment for Decommissioning) Regulations 1999
    (Statutory Instrument No. 2892)

The Environmental Impact Assessment (Scotland) Regulations 1999 (Scottish Statutory Instrument
    No. 1)

In March 1999 SI 1199 was revoked and replaced by the Town and Country Planning (Assessment of Environmental Effects) Regulations 1999 (SI 293), which were accompanied in England by DETR Circular 02/99. The major changes to the system of EIA brought about by these new regulations are:

• more projects automatically require EIA;

• there is more pressure for alternatives to be considered;

- the screening process is more complex but is aided with better advice;

- the screening decision has to be placed on the public register;

- formal scoping opinions can be requested from the local authority;

- the decision on the planning application and the reasons behind it must be made public.

The form of these regulations is very similar to that of the amended EU directive. It has five schedules:

- Schedule 1 lists the projects for which EIA is mandatory;

- Schedule 2 lists projects for which EIA is carried out at the discretion of the local planning authority along with applicable thresholds and criteria;

- Schedule 3 lists the selection criteria which should be used in screening Schedule 2 projects (similar to Annex III of the directive);

- Schedule 4 lists the information which an environmental statement must contain, and that which it should contain (similar to Annex IV of the directive); and

- Schedule 5 lists all the statutory instruments revoked (this list includes all those regulations introduced since 1988 to close various loopholes which had been identified).

The regulations have 35 sections divided between nine parts, preceding the schedules, which give the following information:

Part I (General)

1. Citation, commencement and application
2. Interpretation
3. Prohibition on granting planning permission without consideration of environmental information

Part II (Screening)

4.   General provisions related to screening

5.   Requests for screening opinions of the local planning authority

6.   Requests for screening directions to the Secretary of State

Part III (Procedures concerning applications for planning permissions)

7.   Application made to a local planning authority without an environmental statement

8.   Application referred to the Secretary of State without an environmental statement

9.   Appeal to the Secretary of State without an environmental statement

Part IV (Preparation of environmental statements)

10.   Scoping opinions of the local planning authority

11.   Scoping directions of the Secretary of State

12.   Procedure to facilitate preparation of environmental statements

Part V (Publicity and procedures on submission of environmental statements)

13.   Procedure where an environmental statement is submitted to a local planning authority

14.   Publicity where an environmental statement is submitted after the planning application

15.   Provision of copies of environmental statements and further information for the Secretary of State on referral or appeal

16.   Procedure where an environmental statement is submitted to the Secretary of State

17.   Availability of copies of environmental statements

18.   Charges for copies of environmental statements

19.   Further information and evidence respecting environmental statements

Part VI (Availability of directions etc. and notification of decisions)

20.   Availability of opinions, directions, etc. for inspection

21.   Duties to inform the public and the Secretary of State of final decisions

Part VII (Special cases)

22.   Development by a local planning authority

23. Restriction of grant of permission by old simplified planning zone schemes or enterprise zone orders

24. Restriction of grant of permission by new simplified planning zone schemes or enterprise zone orders

25. Unauthorised development

26. Unauthorised development with significant transboundary effects

Part VIII (Development with significant transboundary effects)

27. Development in England and Wales likely to have significant effects in another member state

28. Projects in another member state likely to have significant transboundary effects

Part IX (Miscellaneous)

29. Service of notices etc.

30. Application to the High Court

31. Hazardous waste and material change of use

32. Extension of the period for an authority's decision on planning application

33. Extension of the power to provide in a development order for the giving of directions as respects the manner in which planning applications are dealt with

34. Revocation of Statutory Instruments and transitional provisions

35. Miscellaneous and consequential amendments

The EIA process resulting from SI 293 is summarised in Figure 5.4.

The action-forcing regulation of SI 293 is regulation 3(2) which states:

> The relevant planning authority or the Secretary of State or an inspector shall not grant planning permission pursuant to an application to which this regulation applies unless they have first taken the environmental information into consideration, and they shall state in their decision that they have done so.

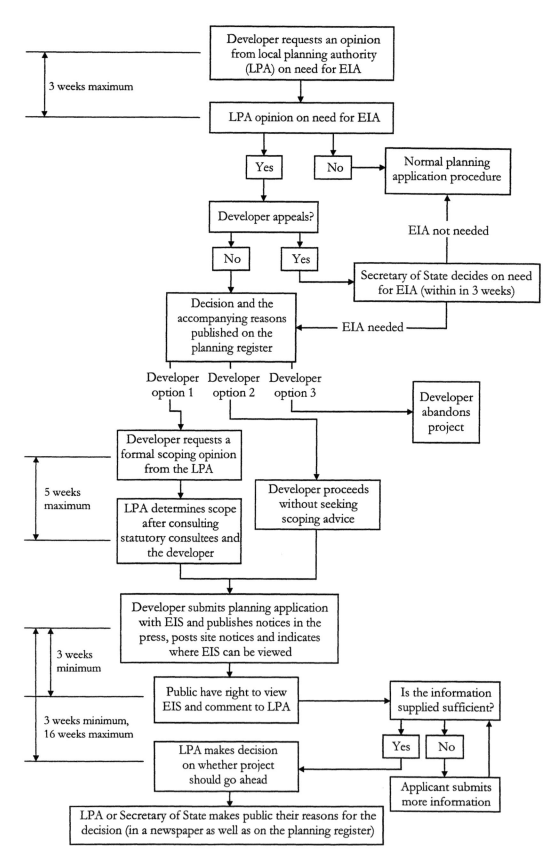

Figure 5.4 EIA procedure in the UK under SI 293 (1999).

5.3.1 Public participation

The 1999 regulations have made it necessary to disclose more information to the public than was previously required, though the level of participation rarely exceeds simply informing the public. The opportunities available to the public are as follows:

- The decision on whether EIA has been requested must be available to the public and, where a planning application is later made, the opinion has to be put on the planning register.

- Where asked for, a scoping opinion must be available to the public and, where a planning application is later made, the opinion has to be put on the planning register.

- The EIS is placed on the planning register which is open to the public. In addition, the public are allowed to purchase a copy of the EIS at a price reflecting the marginal cost of its production. The fact that a planning application accompanied by an EIS has been made must be reported in the local press and by using notices posted at the proposed site. The public have the right to comment on the environmental statement during the first 21 days after it has been submitted along with the planning application. The local planning authority in reaching their decision should then take the comments into consideration. The regulations prevent the local authority, who have 16 weeks to make their decision, from taking less than 21 days to make it.

- Once a decision on the planning application has been made, the decision must be publicised in the local press, and the reasons behind the decision along with a consideration of the mitigation measures must be made available to the public.

5.3.2 Screening

A developer can either choose to carry out an EIA on a voluntary basis, or can ask the local planning authority for a direction. In the latter case, the process followed is stipulated in Part II of the regulations and is illustrated in Figure 5.5. From the time the local authority receives the request for a direction, they have three weeks in which to decide whether an EIA is necessary. They can request more information from the developer if they feel they don't have enough to make a decision. The developer has the right to appeal against the decision (or the lack of a decision). In practice, this would only happen if they were requested to carry out an EIA because of the cost involved. The Secretary of State for the Environment would then have three weeks in which to make a decision, and could again request more information if needed (regulation 6 of SI 293).

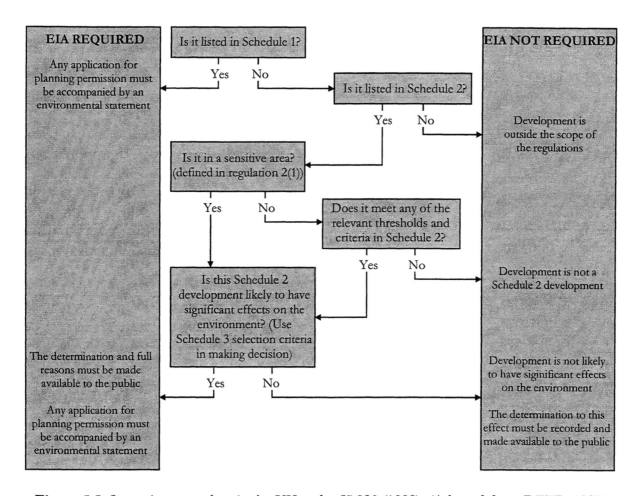

Figure 5.5 Screening procedure in the UK under SI 293 (1999). (Adapted from DETR, 1999.)

Whether the final decision comes from the Secretary of State or the local authority, the developer has to be informed of the decision *with reasons*.

It should also be stressed that there is a chance that a developer might not inform the local authority of their intention to carry out a project until they submit the planning application. At this point, the local authority is required to consider whether the application should be accompanied by an EIS following the same procedure outlined above.

In practice, screening decisions in the early days of the previous regulations were subject to errors because the local planning authorities had a poor understanding of the new regulations and how they really worked. Part of the problem was that, while guidance was published in 1989 (Department of the Environment, 1989), the decision was entirely down to the discretion of the planning authority. The 1999 regulations went through three rounds of consultation and used the results of a research project to help to determine thresholds and indicative criteria to make the decision easier. Schedule 2 indicates minimum thresholds, below which EIA cannot be requested under the regulations. Above these thresholds, the authorities need to make a decision on the significance of the likely impacts, although indicative criteria are provided in Department of the Environment, Transport and the Regions Circular 02/99 (DETR, 1999).

5.3.3   Scoping

Regulation 10 allows a developer to obtain a formal scoping opinion from the planning authority. Enough information has to be provided in order to allow the authority to give such an opinion, and DETR Circular 02/99 even suggests that this information might take the form of a draft EIS.

The planning authority has five weeks to adopt a scoping opinion starting from the date on which the request was received. In producing their opinion, the authority must consult the developer and the statutory consultees.

In formulating a scoping opinion, the authority will inevitably refer to the regulations and associated guidance from the DETR (DETR, 1999). The content of an EIS is specified in Schedule 4 of the regulations and is divided into two parts. Part II indicates the information which will have to be included in the EIS:

1.   A description of the development comprising information on the site, design and size of the development.

2.   A description of the measures envisaged in order to avoid, reduce and, if possible, remedy significant adverse effects.

3.   The data required to identify and assess the main effects which the development is likely to have on the environment.

4.   An outline of the main alternatives studied by the applicant or appellant and an indication of the main reasons for his choice, taking into account the environmental effects.

5.   A non-technical summary of the information provided under paragraphs 1 to 4 of this Part.

Note that paragraph 4 above requires consideration of alternatives studied. Under the previous regulations it clearly was not a requirement that alternatives be studied. Under the new regulations, it is clear that alternatives *which have been considered* must be detailed in an EIS, which potentially means that alternatives do not have to feature in an EIS if the developer chooses not to consider them. On the plus side, the DETR Circular which accompanies the regulations does indicate that consideration of alternatives is widely considered as good practice and includes alternative sites, choice of sites and phasing of construction as alternatives (DETR, 1999, p. 19).

5.3.4   Baseline study

The baseline studies carried out by the developer are at their own discretion – the obligation being to supply certain information within the EIS and to give an indication of how the information was obtained. The regulations make no attempt to constrain the developer in any way over their particular information-gathering approaches.

5.3.5   Impact prediction and assessment

The techniques used by the authors of an environmental statement are left entirely to their own discretion. It is clear from the regulations that impacts on human beings, flora, fauna, soil, water, air, climate, landscape, material assets including architectural and archaeological heritage and the interaction between any of these have to be considered, but no further advice is forthcoming.

The guidance document produced by the DETR (DETR, 1999) does suggest that EIS authors might like to look at a *Good Practice Guide* previously published by the DETR. This guide (DETR, 1995) is a 134-page book with separate sections for each of the impact types.

5.3.6   Mitigation

The regulations make it clear that the content of the decision made on the project, along with a description (if the application has been approved) of the mitigation measures, must be placed on the planning register which is a public document (paragraph 126 of the regulations).

The associated guidance does have more to say on the subject of mitigation measures and indicates that consideration should be given as to how mitigation measures can be secured (DETR, 1999, p. 26). The guidance suggests that planning conditions can be used to require a scheme of mitigation measures be submitted to the planning authority for approval prior to the development going ahead. Alternatively, section 106 of the Town and Country Planning Act 1990 can be used to obtain a planning obligation (known previously as agreements or referred to as means of obtaining 'planning gain').

5.3.7   The environmental impact statement

It is clearly stipulated that it is the developer's responsibility to prepare an environmental statement. What should go in an EIS has been dealt with in section 5.3.3 above.

There is some stipulation of the numbers of EISs to be submitted – four need to be given to the local authority so that the authority can send three to the Secretary of State. In addition, the applicants need to supply enough extra sets of the EIS so that one can be handed to each of the statutory consultees.

In terms of availability to the public, it was a concern under the previous regulations that charges made were too high. The new regulations say that the applicant must make copies available either free or at a cost representing printing and distribution. This is a clear indication that the public should only be charged for the marginal cost of EIS production and not for the total cost! Further to this, the developers are 'encouraged' to publish the non-technical summary as a separate document and have it available for free.

5.3.8   EIS review

The UK legislation has no provision for the independent review of environmental statements. The local authority uses the statements as material evidence in determining planning applications; if they feel that the information is deficient in some areas (and they are required to ensure that the EIS contains all the information listed in Part II of Schedule 4), they have the right to request more information. However, the authority does not have the power to refuse planning permission on the basis of a poor quality environmental statement: if it complies with the procedural requirements of the legislation then it has to be accepted and used.

5.3.9   Monitoring and post-development audit

As for review, there are no provisions in UK legislation for monitoring of any kind to take place after the development has been constructed. However, a local planning authority does have the means to impose conditions on the granting of planning permission via the Town and Country Planning Act 1990 and, therefore, can require monitoring activities to take place where it is a reasonable request.

5.3.10   Was the implementation of the directive complete and on time?

The UK government implemented the 1985 directive covering projects within the remit of planning a few weeks late. However, the 1997 amendments (for projects falling within the remit of planning) were implemented with two days to spare before the deadline specified in the directive itself.

As for being complete, while SI 293 seems to comply with the amended directive, amendments are already due to allow for old mining permissions as discussed previously. The regulations allow for the fact that 'permitted developments' (mentioned earlier in this section) avoid the need for a planning application by specifically removing the 'permitted development' status of all project types mentioned in Schedule 1, and all project types mentioned in Schedule 2 which are deemed to have potentially significant effects.

5.4   Case law related to EIA

This section will concentrate on the case law which has developed over the use of EIA legislation within the United Kingdom. The cases have mainly involved parties seeking judicial review of decisions involving environmental impact assessment. We will also briefly examine some European Court rulings on environmental assessment.

5.4.1   UK case law

The occasions for justifying court action with respect to environmental assessment legislation are limited. One area which does cause some controversy is the screening decision where, you will remember, the competent authority has the discretion to decide which Schedule 2 projects will require EIA. The first court challenge came in 1991 with the case of *R* v. *Swale Borough Council and Medway Ports Authority, ex parte The Royal Society for the Protection of Birds*. The case is listed in this format because, in a judicial review, the case is always brought by the crown on behalf of (this is where the 'ex parte' bit of the case title fits in) whoever it is – in this case the RSPB.

The facts in this particular case are that planning permission was granted by Swale Borough Council to allow Medway Ports Authority to reclaim a 125-acre site known as Lappel Bank near the mouth of the Medway. The Medway estuary at that particular point is an important area both nationally and internationally for supporting migratory birds. Indeed, the whole area around and including Lappel Bank was a candidate for designation as a Ramsar site (under the Ramsar Convention on Wetlands of International Importance) and a Special Protection Area (under the EC Directive on the Conservation of Wild Birds). Despite this, the Nature Conservancy Council had no objections to the proposed development.

Medway Ports Authority needed the 125-acre site as a short-term storage area for import/export cargoes which would be transported via Sheerness Docks – a major source of employment for the Isle of Sheppey, Kent's highest area of unemployment.

The case was a judicial review with the RSPB claiming that the borough council had acted beyond its powers. The case was not simply about the screening decision; rather the challenge was over the granting of planning permission by Swale Borough Council. The RSPB were of the opinion that the proper procedures were not followed and, in particular, that no environmental impact assessment had taken place despite the fact that, in their opinion, the project approved fitted into either Schedule 1 or Schedule 2.

The judge felt that the decision as to whether any particular development was or was not within Schedule 1 or Schedule 2 of the relevant regulations was a question of fact and degree, not of law; it could not therefore be held that the decision of the borough council had been wrong. He went on to say that it was not obvious from reading through Schedule 2 that the planning application required environmental assessment because the council were simply using their judgement to say that the environmental effects would not be significant.

From this case, it appears that the competent authority will be given a large amount of discretion by the courts in making their screening decisions.

Another relevant case is that of *R* v. *Poole Borough Council, ex parte Beebee and others* (1991). In this particular case, Beebee is the name of a particular person belonging to one of the organisations in question.

In this instance, Poole Borough Council granted themselves planning permission for housing development on part of Canford Heath, but in doing so had not considered whether environmental assessment was required or not. It is interesting to note that, initially, the judges had to decide whether the applicants seeking judicial review had sufficient standing to be able to bring the case. In Latin, this issue of having sufficient standing is known as *locus standi*. It seems that it is a very difficult decision to make as to whether a person or group have sufficient standing to bring a case if they do not actually own the land to be developed. In this case, they were held to have sufficient standing because:

*   of their long association with the site;

*   their financial input into the site; and

*   their name was mentioned with respect to the planning permission which was obtained.

The council had not considered the need for environmental assessment for this application, and did not dispute that this was true. The fact that the council did not feel the effects to be significant should be irrelevant in this case because the issue was whether the council ever even considered that point at all. They admitted that they hadn't.

The judge came out with the extraordinary conclusion that the existing planning process had already provided the authority with all the information which would have been provided by an environmental statement and, therefore, there was no need to quash the planning permission on this basis. This conclusion makes it fairly clear that the judge did not understand the EIA regulations or the aims of environmental assessment to provide a systematic means of producing all the required information to aid a decision-maker! Such a view on the decision in this case has been echoed by others (see, for example, Sheate, 1996, pp. 126–7).

The next case to examine is one which was highly controversial at the time as it concerns the M3 extension through Twyford Down. The relevant case is *Twyford Parish Council and Others* v. *Secretary of State for Transport* (1992).

The argument centres around the interpretation of the provisions for environmental assessment regarding the date on which projects should have been covered by them. In this case, planning permission had not been given for the M3 extension when the environmental assessment regulations were passed, but the application had been made. Twyford Parish Council and others, who were trying to get the planning permission quashed, interpreted the Environmental Assessment Directive as clearly stating that consent should not be given after 3 July 1988 for projects which were subject to environmental impact assessment in accordance with the directive.

The Department of Transport argued that the directive was not intended to apply to projects already in the pipeline, i.e. ones for which the planning application had already been made, by 3 July 1988. They backed this up by reasoning that a local inquiry had already taken place and it was senseless to nullify this and start again.

The judges concluded that the Department of Transport were correct in their interpretation as the idea of environmental assessment was to take account of environmental effects of development projects at the earliest possible stage, and for large projects such as this already in the pipeline, it was surely unreasonable to expect the environmental assessment process to be applied.

Along the same lines, Sheate (1996) refers to the case of *Lewin and Rowley* v. *Secretary of State for the Environment and Secretary of State for Transport* (1989). Lewin and Rowley objected to a draft order for the A1–M1 link road which would cross the historic site of the Battle of Naseby. However, a public inquiry had been held into the scheme between 1984 and 1985, the Inspector's report was published in July 1986, the Secretary of State's decision letter was given on 6 April 1987 and the definitive order was made on 20 December 1987 to come into force on 5 February 1988. Clearly this is not a 'pipeline' project though Lewin and Rowley argued that development consent could not be deemed to have been given until the statutory appeal against the order had been determined or until contract for the work had been placed. The Court of Appeal disagreed and pointed out that the courts were not competent authorities (that is, the courts are not the body given the power to make decisions on such matters under the law – the Secretaries of State had that power; the courts can only overturn decisions when something has been decided which is not within the authority granted by the law).

Another case to refer to is that of the *Petition of Kincardine and Deeside District Council* brought in 1991. The facts in the case are that the owners of a site applied to the Forestry Commission for a grant under the Woodland Grant Scheme for planting trees in an area over 800 hectares in size. The area in question was within the boundaries of Deeside District Council and they sought judicial review on the grounds that the Forestry Commission should have examined whether an environmental assessment was required, and that they failed to do so.

The relevant EIA regulations are the Environmental Assessment (Afforestation) Regulations 1988 (SI No. 1207) which came into force on 15 July 1988. They therefore require that any application for a grant or loan in respect of afforestation projects received on or after this date is subject to the regulations. An initial application for a grant was received on 13 July 1988, and despite the fact that alterations were subsequently made, the court was happy that this was the application date and, therefore, the regulations did not apply.

This is not the end of the story as the EC directive was required to come into force on 3 July 1988. The question raised in this case was, therefore, did the directive have direct effect in this matter? (For a definition of direct effect, refer back to section 3.3.1.) Theoretically, if the provisions in the directive are unconditional and sufficiently precise, then the directive should have direct effect and the relevant date for consideration of whether environmental assessment was required by the Forestry Commission was 3 July.

A few issues were examined by the court:

- whether the time limit for implementation of the directive is sufficiently precise;

- whether the obligations of the directive regarding the requirement for EIA of afforestation projects are sufficiently precise and unconditional to impose direct effect in this situation.

In answering the first question, the court felt that the date by which the directive should have been implemented was unconditional. They then went on to find that for Annex I projects, the directive was sufficiently precise and unconditional to have direct effect and confer rights on individuals in the UK. However, at the same time, they felt that the wording of the directive in relation to Annex II projects (which this one falls under) was not sufficiently unconditional and precise to have direct effect.

As in the Twyford Down case, the judicial review failed to overturn the decisions made by the competent authorities exercising their duties with regard to environmental impact assessment.

An issue which has also been clarified to some extent in the courts is that of what constitutes an improvement as opposed to a separate project – or when should several smaller projects be considered as parts of one large project? Clearly there are implications for EIA! *R v. Secretary of State for Transport, ex parte Surrey County Council* (1993) was an application to the High Court for judicial review of the decision by the Department of Transport to consider proposals to widen the M25 up to 14 lanes in some parts of Surrey as a series of separate schemes. Surrey County Council argued that it should be considered as one large scheme. The High Court refused their application for judicial review because an EIA had not yet been carried out – but they did accept the argument, and stated that they would expect the EIS to consider all the development plans for the M25.

A more recent case, again involving judicial review, has hinged over the right of third parties to have the reasons for not requiring environmental assessment made clear to them. The case in question, *R v. Secretary of State for the Environment, Transport and the Regions and Parcelforce, ex parte Marson* was heard in the Court of Appeal in May 1998 (Macrory, 1998). The case concerned a proposed development near Coventry Airport by Parcelforce within the Green Belt. The project itself fell within Schedule 2 of the UK regulations and was contentious enough for local residents to ask the Secretary of State to call in the project for decision, or at least to insist on EIA being carried out. Having received more information from Parcelforce, the Secretary of State decided not to call in the application and directed that environmental assessment was not required. No reasons were given for this direction other than repeating the text of the regulations alongside an opinion that the project 'would not be likely to have significant effects on the environment' (Macrory, 1998).

A local resident sought judicial review on the grounds that he was entitled to full reasons for the decision. This application was refused by the High Court and was then referred to the Court of Appeal. The judges felt that the legislation, both the EIA directive and UK regulations, was clear in that they require that reasons be provided where an environmental assessment is required, but not where EIA is not required. In coming to this conclusion, the Court of Appeal looked not only at the law, but also referred to general standards of fairness. The conclusion was that the Secretary of State is entitled to exercise discretion in such a case and had given the reasons for this discretion, i.e. that effects would not be significant.

The result of this case is that developers are entitled to receive full reasons for a decision that environmental assessment is required in the UK, but members of the public are not entitled to hear reasons why environmental assessment is not required (Macrory, 1998). Macrory (1998) discusses the further implications of this decision and says that:

> The principle will also apply to local authorities and other governmental bodies which make similar decisions, and reflects a degree of distortion in the planning system.

There was a House of Lords ruling in February 1999 relating to a North Yorkshire quarry which had received planning conditions in 1947. The UK government's line on this had been that, as no development consent was required for a reactivation of this consent, EIA did not apply. The House of Lords, however, did not agree and they ruled that the granting of updated planning conditions constituted development consent. As a result, the government is having to bring in new regulations to cover all planning consents of this type granted before the EIA regulations came into force back in 1988 (Anon., 1999). This particular case therefore has significance for the Interim Development Orders mentioned on p. 123.

Finally, the High Court ruled in April 1999, in the case of *R. v. St Edmundsbury Borough Council, ex parte Walton*, that a local authority had incorrectly approved a road scheme without first carrying out environmental assessment (Macrory, 1999a). The story behind the case is that Greene King Brewery wished to build an access road to its brewery depot in Bury St Edmunds. The idea of the road was to reduce congestion in the town, but the route ran across meadows of both local amenity and historical importance. The application for the development was not accompanied by an environmental impact statement and the development falls under Annex II of the 1985 directive. The local authority had made a conscious decision that no EIA was needed, and the decision was made by a planning officer. The case brought against the authority was based on the fact that while local authorities do have the power to delegate decisions on whether EIA should be required for Annex II projects to its officers, there was no formal written delegation. The court agreed that the delegation of a duty like this should be made formally in writing because of the importance of the decision. The court then went on to consider whether the planning committee might have reached a different decision if it had an environmental statement to read as well and concluded that it might have. As a result, both the decision not to ask for an EIA and the planning decision were quashed.

The implications of the last case to be discussed are that, as well as local authorities having to check the rigour of their delegation procedures (Macrory, 1999a), the courts now accept that EIA presents environmental information which is needed in order to make valid decisions.

5.4.2   European case law on EIA

The first case to be considered in the European Court of Justice on EIA concerned the German EIA procedures. In common with some of the UK case law we have looked at, this case stemmed from whether EIA should have been carried out for two projects in Bavaria for which consent had been sought in September 1988 and November 1989 respectively (Macrory, 1994). The German EIA law was not implemented until August 1990, and so these two projects were held not to require EIA. However, as we know, the EC Directive on Environmental Assessment should have been implemented by 3 July 1988.

The European Court of Justice ruled that the German law failed to comply with the directive in so far as it was implemented far too late.

This is a clear indication that projects for which planning consent was sought between 3 July 1988 and 15 July 1988 have not followed the requirements of the EC directive in the UK. It does not, however, address the question of whether projects for which planning consent was sought before 3 July, but were not approved before that date, also fail to comply with the directive.

Sheate (1996) does report, however, that the European Court of Justice has now twice ruled (contradicting the view of the European Commission) that it is the date of application for consent, not the date of consent, which is important. In the case of *Commission* v. *Federal Republic of Germany* (Case C431/92) the court specifically said:

> The date when the application for consent was formally lodged thus constitutes the sole criterion which may be used. Such a criterion accords with the principles of legal certainty and is designed to safeguard the effectiveness of the Directive.
>
> (Judgement of the Court, 11 August 1995)

There was a court case in the Court at First Instance of the European Communities – that of *Greenpeace* v. *Commission of the European Communities* (1996) in which Greenpeace and 18 other applicants brought an action under Article 173 of the Treaty of Rome. They argued over a decision of the Commission to use regional funds to aid the construction of two electricity power stations in the Canary Islands; the work started without an environmental assessment being carried out as required by Directive 85/337/EEC. The Commission fought the case by arguing that Greenpeace and the other applicants didn't have *locus standi*, i.e. they weren't sufficiently affected themselves.

The court found that the applicants lacked *locus standi* and so the real question of the court case – whether the European Commission itself bypassed Directive 85/337/EEC illegally – was not considered. Greenpeace are understood to have appealed to the European Court of Justice (Anon., 1996).

It was also reported on this case that

> the courts have shown themselves to be out of step with mainstream thinking emanating from DG XI of the Commission itself. In the Green Paper on Environmental Impairment and on several other occasions the Commission has asserted the collective interest in environmental protection, and has suggested that, in respect of the unowned environment, there ought to be mechanisms by which interest groups can pursue actions on behalf of the environment.
>
> (Anon., 1996)

Macrory (1997) reports that in a case originating from the Netherlands, the scope of the 1985 directive was broadened. The facts of the case are that a local zoning plan was modified in connection with the reinforcement of dykes. No environmental assessment was carried out because the proposed works fell below statutory thresholds for Annex II projects set by Dutch law. The applicants to the European Court of Justice argued that the works should have been subjected to environmental assessment and they were supported in this by the European Commission.

The court ruled that member states did have discretion to set thresholds, but that this was not unlimited discretion – if the outcome of the threshold was to exclude whole types of projects, then this was unacceptable. In addition, the proposed project was a modification and the Dutch government argued that it was only modifications to Annex I projects which fell under obligations imposed by the directive. The court disagreed with this view and interpreted the scope of the directive as applying to modification of all Annex II as well as Annex I projects.

Finally, Macrory (1999b) reports on a case in September 1999 which has extended the scope of the directive on EIA yet further (note that this case refers to Directive 85/337/EEC, not the amended version). The case, *World Wildlife Fund and Others* v. *Autonome Provinz Bozen and Others,* was a challenge to the validity of a decision to approve a project to convert a former military airfield into a commercial airport in Italy. An environmental statement produced for the project in 1996 didn't comply with the directive and no one disputed this. The issue considered by the court was whether Italian legislation was allowed to exempt projects of this nature from requirements for EIA. The project fell under Annex II of the directive, and Italian legislation stipulated that extensions or alterations to existing airports where the runway exceeded 2,100 metres required EIA. In this case the runway extension was shorter than this, and the Italian legislation stated that EIA would be required for other projects where they exceeded thresholds listed in the regulations by 20% – but there was no threshold for airport extensions and modifications. As such, this project was exempted from requiring EIA under Italian law!

The court found that this was not acceptable – the directive did not allow exemption of projects from Annex II in advance. In this case, there would need to have been some means of assessing the significance of the impacts in order to make a decision – even if this were done through thresholds set in advance. The court also made it clear that the directive did have direct effect (see section 3.3.1) and that individuals could rely on the directive in cases where member states had exceeded the discretion given to them.

APPENDIX 1

DIRECTIVE 85/337/EEC (AS AMENDED BY DIRECTIVE 97/11/EC)

INFORMAL CONSOLIDATION OF DIRECTIVE 85/337/EEC

on the assessment of the effects of certain public and private projects on the environment as amended by Council Directive 97/11/EC

Adopted by Council 3 March 1997

THE COUNCIL OF THE EUROPEAN UNION,

Having regard to the Treaty establishing the European Community, and in particular Article 130s(1) thereof,

Having regard to the proposal from the Commission[1]

Having regard to the opinion of the Economic and Social Committee[2]

Having regard to the opinion of the Committee of the Regions[3]

Acting in accordance with the procedure laid down in Article 189c of the Treaty[4]

1.   Whereas Council Directive 85/337/EEC of 27 June 1985 on the assessment of the effects of certain public and private projects on the environment[5] aims at providing the competent authorities with relevant information to enable them to take a decision on a specific project in full knowledge of the project's likely significant impact on the environment; whereas the assessment procedure is a fundamental instrument of environmental policy as defined in Article 130r of the Treaty and of the Fifth Community Programme of policy and action in relation to the environment and sustainable development;

2.   Whereas, pursuant to Article 130r(2) of the Treaty, Community policy on the environment is based on the precautionary principle and on the principle that preventive action should be taken, that environmental damage should as a priority be rectified at source and that the polluter should pay;

3.   Whereas the main principles of the assessment of environmental effects should be harmonized and whereas the Member States may lay down stricter rules to protect the environment;

4.   Whereas experience acquired in environmental impact assessment, as recorded in the report on the implementation of Directive 85/337/EEC, adopted by the Commission on 2 April 1993, shows that it is necessary to introduce provisions designed to clarify, supplement and improve the rules on the assessment procedure, in order to ensure that the Directive is applied in an increasingly harmonized and efficient manner;

5.   Whereas projects for which an assessment is required should be subject to a requirement for development consent; whereas the assessment should be carried out before such consent is granted;

6.   Whereas it is appropriate to make additions to the list of projects which have significant effects on the environment and which must on that account as a rule be made subject to systematic assessment;

7.   Whereas projects of other types may not have significant effects on the environment in every case; whereas these projects should be assessed where Member States consider they are likely to have significant effects on the environment;

8. Whereas Member States may set thresholds or criteria for the purpose of determining which such projects should be subject to assessment on the basis of the significance of their environmental effects; whereas Member States should not be required to examine projects below those thresholds or outside those criteria on a case-by-case basis;

9. Whereas when setting such thresholds or criteria or examining projects on a case-by-case basis for the purpose of determining which projects should be subject to assessment on the basis of their significant environmental effects, Member States should take account of the relevant selection criteria set out in this Directive; whereas, in accordance with the subsidiarity principle, the Member States are in the best position to apply these criteria in specific instances;

10. Whereas the existence of a location criterion referring to special protection areas designated by Member States pursuant to Council Directive 79/409/EEC of 2 April 1979 on the conservation of wild birds[6] and 92/43/EEC of 21 May 1992 on the conservation of natural habitats and of wild fauna and flora[7] does not imply necessarily that projects in those areas are to be automatically subject to an assessment under this Directive;

11. Whereas it is appropriate to introduce a procedure in order to enable the developer to obtain an opinion from the competent authorities on the content and extent of the information to be elaborated and supplied for the assessment; whereas Member States, in the framework of this procedure, may require the developer to provide, *inter alia*, alternatives for the projects for which it intends to submit an application;

12. Whereas it is desirable to strengthen the provisions concerning environmental impact assessment in a transboundary context to take account of developments at international level;

13. Whereas the Community signed the Convention on Environmental Impact Assessment in a Transboundary Context on 25 February 1991,

HAS ADOPTED THIS DIRECTIVE:

Article 1

1.   This Directive shall apply to the assessment of the environmental effects of those public and private projects which are likely to have significant effects on the environment.

2.   For the purposes of this Directive:

'project' means:

–   the execution of construction works or of other installations of schemes,

–   other interventions in the natural surroundings and landscape including those involving the extraction of mineral resources;

'developer' means:

the applicant for authorisation for a private project or the public authority which initiates a project;

'development consent' means:

the decision of the competent authority or authorities which entitled the developer to proceed with the project.

3.   The competent authority or authorities shall be that or those which the Member States designate as responsible for performing the duties arising from this Directive.

4.   Projects serving national defence purposes are not covered by this Directive.

5.   This Directive shall not apply to projects the details of which are adopted by a specific act of national legislation, since the objectives of this Directive, including that of supplying information, are achieved through the legislative process.

Article 2

1.   Member States shall adopt all measures necessary to ensure that, before consent is given, projects likely to have significant effects on the environment by virtue, *inter alia*, of their nature, size or location are made subject to a requirement for development consent and an assessment with regard to their effects. These projects are defined in Article 4.

2.   The environmental impact assessment may be integrated into the existing procedures for consent to projects in the Member States, or, failing this, into other procedures or into procedures to be established to comply with the aims of this Directive.

    a)   Member States may provide a single procedure in order to fulfil the requirements of this Directive and the requirements of Council Directive 96/61/EC of 24 September 1996 on integrated pollution prevention and control.[8]

3.   Without prejudice to Article 7, Member States may, in exceptional cases, exempt a specific project in whole or in part from the provisions laid down in this Directive.

In this event, the Member States shall:

    (a)   consider whether another form of assessment would be appropriate and whether the information thus collected should be made available to the public;

    (b)   make available to the public concerned, the information relating to the exemption and the reasons for granting it;

    (c)   inform the Commission, prior to granting consent, of the reasons justifying the exemption granted, and provide it with the information made available, where applicable to their own nationals.

The Commission shall immediately forward the documents received to the other Member States.

The Commission shall report annually to the Council on the application of this paragraph.

Article 3

The environmental impact assessment shall identify, describe and assess in an appropriate manner, in the light of each individual case and in accordance with Articles 4 to 11, the direct and indirect effects of a project on the following factors:

- human beings, fauna and flora;
- soil, water, air, climate and the landscape;
- material assets and the cultural heritage;
- the interaction between the factors mentioned in the first, second and third indents.

Article 4

1. Subject to Article 2(3), projects listed in Annex I shall be made subject to an assessment in accordance with Articles 5 to 10.

2. Subject to Article 2(3), for projects listed in Annex II, the Member States shall determine through:

    (a) a case-by-case examination;

         or

    (b) thresholds or criteria set by the Member State

    whether the project shall be made subject to an assessment in accordance with Articles 5 to 10.

    Member States may decide to apply both procedures referred to in (a) and (b).

3. When a case-by-case examination is carried out or thresholds or criteria are set for the purpose of paragraph 2, the relevant selection criteria set out in Annex III shall be taken into account.

4. Member States shall ensure that the determination made by the competent authorities under paragraph 2 is made available to the public.

Article 5

1.   In the case of projects which, pursuant to Article 4, must be subjected to an environmental impact assessment in accordance with Articles 5 to 10, Member States shall adopt the necessary measures to ensure that the developer supplies in an appropriate form the information specified in Annex IV inasmuch as:

   (a)   the Member States consider that the information is relevant to a given stage of the consent procedure and to the specific characteristics of a particular project or type of project and of the environmental features likely to be affected;

   (b)   the Member States consider that a developer may reasonably be required to compile this information having regard *inter alia* to current knowledge and methods of assessment.

2.   Member States shall take the necessary measures to ensure that, if the developer so requests before submitting an application for development consent, the competent authority shall give an opinion on the information to be supplied by the developer in accordance with paragraph 1. The competent authority shall consult the developer and authorities referred to in Article 6(1) before it gives its opinion.

   The fact that the authority has given an opinion under this paragraph shall not preclude it from subsequently requiring the developer to submit further information.

   Member States may require the competent authorities to give such an opinion, irrespective of whether the developer so requests.

3.   The information to be provided by the developer in accordance with paragraph 1 shall include at least:

   –   a description of the project comprising information on the site, design and size of the project;

   –   a description of the measures envisaged in order to avoid, reduce and, if possible, remedy significant adverse effects;

   –   the data required to identify and assess the main effects which the project is likely to have on the environment;

–   an outline of the main alternatives studied by the developer and an indication of the main reasons for his choice, taking into account the environmental effects;

–   a non-technical summary of the information mentioned in the previous indents.

4.   Member States shall, if necessary, ensure that any authorities holding relevant information, with particular reference to Article 3, make this information available to the developer.

Article 6

1.   Member States shall take the measures necessary to ensure that the authorities likely to be concerned by the project by reason of their specific environmental responsibilities are given an opportunity to express their opinion on the information supplied by the developer and on the request for development consent. To this end, Member States shall designate the authorities to be consulted, either in general terms or on a case-by-case basis. The information gathered pursuant to Article 5 shall be forwarded to those authorities. Detailed arrangements for consultation shall be laid down by the Member States.

2.   Member States shall ensure that any request for development consent and any information gathered pursuant to Article 5 are made available to the public within a reasonable time, in order to give the public concerned the opportunity to express an opinion before the development consent is granted.

3.   The detailed arrangements for such information and consultation shall be determined by the Member States, which may in particular, depending on the particular characteristics of the projects or sites concerned:

–   determine the public concerned;

–   specify the places where the information can be consulted;

–   specify the way in which the public may be informed, for example, by bill-posting within a certain radius, publication in local newspapers, organisation of exhibitions with plans, drawings, tables, graphs, models;

–   determine the manner in which the public is to be consulted, for example, by written submissions, by public enquiry;

    −   fix appropriate time limits for the various stages of the procedure in order to ensure that a decision is taken within a reasonable period.

Article 7

1.   Where a Member State is aware that a project is likely to have significant effects on the environment in another Member State or where a Member State likely to be significantly affected so requests, the Member State in whose territory the project is intended to be carried out shall send to the affected Member State as soon as possible and no later than when informing its own public, *inter alia*:

    (a)   a description of the project, together with any available information on its possible transboundary impact;

    (b)   information on the nature of the decision which may be taken,

and shall give the other Member State a reasonable time in which to indicate whether it wishes to participate in the Environmental Impact Assessment procedure, and may include the information referred to in paragraph 2.

2.   If a Member State which receives information pursuant to paragraph 1 indicates that it intends to participate in the Environmental Impact Assessment procedure, the Member State in whose territory the project is intended to be carried out shall, if it has not already done so, send to the affected Member State the information gathered pursuant to Article 5 and relevant information regarding the said procedure, including the request for development consent.

3.   The Member States concerned, each insofar as it is concerned, shall also:

    (a)   arrange for the information referred to in paragraphs 1 and 2 to be made available, within a reasonable time, to the authorities referred to in Article 6(1) and the public concerned in the territory of the Member State likely to be significantly affected; and

    (b)   ensure that those authorities and the public concerned are given an opportunity, before development consent for the project is granted, to forward their opinion within a reasonable time on the information supplied to the competent authority in the Member State in whose territory the project is intended to be carried out.

4.   The Member States concerned shall enter into consultations concerning, *inter alia*, the potential transboundary effects of the project and the measures envisaged to reduce or eliminate such effects and shall agree on a reasonable timeframe for the duration of the consultation period.

5.   The detailed arrangements for implementing the provisions of this Article may be determined by the Member States concerned.

Article 8

The results of consultations and the information gathered pursuant to Articles 5, 6 and 7 must be taken into consideration in the development consent procedure.

Article 9

1.   When a decision to grant or refuse development consent has been taken, the competent authority or authorities shall inform the public thereof in accordance with the appropriate procedures and shall make available to the public the following information:
    –   the content of the decision and any conditions attached thereto;
    –   the main reasons and considerations on which the decision is based;
    –   a description, where necessary, of the main measures to avoid, reduce and, if possible, offset the major adverse effects.

2.   The competent authority or authorities shall inform any Member State which has been consulted pursuant to Article 7, forwarding to it the information referred to in paragraph 1.

Article 10

The provisions of this Directive shall not affect the obligation on the competent authorities to respect the limitations imposed by national regulations and administrative provisions and accepted legal practices with regard to commercial and industrial confidentiality, including intellectual property, and the safeguarding of the public interest.

Where Article 7 applies, the transmission to another Member State and the receipt of information by another Member State shall be subject to the limitations in force in the Member State in which the project is proposed.

Article 11

1.   The Member States and the Commission shall exchange information on the experience gained in applying this Directive.

2.   In particular, Member States shall inform the Commission of any criteria and/or thresholds adopted for the selection of the projects in question, in accordance with Article 4(2).

3.   Five years after notification of this Directive, the Commission shall send the European Parliament and the Council a report on its application and effectiveness. The report shall be based on the aforementioned exchange of information.

4.   On the basis of this exchange of information, the Commission shall submit to the Council additional proposals, should this be necessary, with a view to this Directive being applied in a sufficiently coordinated manner.

Article 12

1.   Member States shall take the measures necessary to comply with this Directive within three years of its notification.

2.   Member States shall communicate to the Commission the texts of the provisions of national law which they adopt in the field covered by this Directive.

Article 2 (of Common Position)

Five years after the entry into force of this Directive, the Commission shall send the European Parliament and the Council a report on the application and effectiveness of Directive 85/337/EEC as amended by this Directive. The report shall be based on the exchange of information provided for by Article 11(1) and (2).

On the basis of this report, the Commission shall, where appropriate, submit to the Council additional proposals with a view to ensuring further coordination in the application of this Directive.

Article 3 (of Common Position)

1. Member States shall bring into force the laws, regulations and administrative provisions necessary to comply with this Directive by 14 March 1999 at the latest. They shall forthwith inform the Commission thereof.

    When Member States adopt these provisions, these shall contain a reference to this Directive or shall be accompanied by such reference at the time of their official publication. The procedure for such reference shall be adopted by Member States.

2. If a request for development consent is submitted to a competent authority before the end of the time limit laid down in paragraph 1, the provisions of Directive 85/337/EEC prior to these amendments shall continue to apply.

Article 4 (of Common Position)

This Directive shall enter into force on the twentieth day following that of its publication in the *Official Journal of the European Communities*.

Article 5 (of Common Position)

This Directive is addressed to the Member States.

ANNEX I

Projects subject to Article 4(1)

1.   Crude-oil refineries (excluding undertakings manufacturing only lubricants from crude oil) and installations for the gasification and liquefaction of 500 tonnes or more of coal or bituminous shale per day.

2.   –   Thermal power stations and other combustion installations with a heat output of 300 megawatts or more, and

–   nuclear power stations and other nuclear reactors including the dismantling or decommissioning of such power stations or reactors* (except research installations for the production and conversion of fissionable and fertile materials, whose maximum power does not exceed 1 kilowatt continuous thermal load).

3.   (a)   Installations for the reprocessing of irradiated nuclear fuel.

(b)   Installations designed:

– for the production or enrichment of nuclear fuel,
– for the processing of irradiated nuclear fuel or high-level radioactive waste,
– for the final disposal of irradiated nuclear fuel,
– solely for the final disposal of radioactive waste,
– solely for the storage (planned for more than 10 years) of irradiated nuclear fuels or radioactive waste in a different site than the production site.

---

* Nuclear power stations and other nuclear reactors cease to be such an installation when all nuclear fuel and other radioactively contaminated elements have been removed permanently from the installation site.

4.   –   Integrated works for the initial smelting of cast-iron and steel;

      –   Installations for the production of non-ferrous crude metals from ore, concentrates or secondary raw materials by metallurgical, chemical or electrolytic processes.

5.   Installations for the extraction of asbestos and for the processing and transformation of asbestos and products containing asbestos: for asbestos-cement products, with an annual production of more than 20 000 tonnes of finished products, for friction material, with an annual production of more than 50 tonnes of finished products, and for other uses of asbestos, utilization of more than 200 tonnes per year.

6.   Integrated chemical installations, i.e. those installations for the manufacture on an industrial scale of substances using chemical conversion processes, in which several units are juxtaposed and are functionally linked to one another and which are:

      (i)   the production of basic organic chemicals;

      (ii)   for the production of basic inorganic chemicals;

      (iii) for the production of phosphorous-, nitrogen- or potassium-based fertilizers (simple or compound fertilizers)

      (iv)   for the production of basic plant health products and of biocides;

      (v)   for the production of basic pharmaceutical products using a chemical or biological process;

      (vi)   for the production of explosives.

7.   (a)   Construction of lines for long-distance railway traffic and of airports[9] with a basic runway length of 2100 m or more;

      (b)   Construction of motorways and express roads;[10]

      (c)   Construction of a new road of four or more lanes, or realignment and/or widening of an existing road of two lanes or less so as to provide four or more lanes, where such new road, or realigned and/or widened section of road would be 10 km or more in a continuous length.

8. (a) Inland waterways and ports for inland-waterway traffic which permit the passage of vessels of over 1350 tonnes;

    (b) Trading ports, piers for loading and unloading connected to land and outside ports (excluding ferry piers) which can take vessels of over 1350 tonnes.

    (c) (1) For the purposes of this Directive, 'airport' means airports which comply with the definition in the 1944 Chicago Convention setting up the International Civil Aviation Organization (Annex 14).

         (2) For the purposes of the Directive, 'express road' means a road which complies with the definition in the European Agreement on Main International Traffic Arteries of 15 November 1975.

9. Waste disposal installations for the incineration, chemical treatment as defined in Annex IIA to Directive 75/442/EEC (1) under heading D9, or landfill of hazardous waste (i.e. waste to which Directive 91/689/EEC (2) applies).

10. Waste disposal installations for the incineration or chemical treatment as defined in Annex IIA to Directive 75/442/EEC under heading D9 of non-hazardous waste with a capacity exceeding 100 tonnes per day.

11. Groundwater abstraction or artificial groundwater recharge schemes where the annual volume of water abstracted or recharged is equivalent to or exceeds 10 million cubic metres.

12. (a) Works for the transfer of water resources between river basins where this transfer aims at preventing possible shortages of water and where the amount of water transferred exceeds 100 million cubic metres/year;

     (b) In all other cases, works for the transfer of water resources between river basins where the multi-annual average flow of the basin of abstraction exceeds 2000 million cubic metres/year and where the amount of water transferred exceeds 5% of this flow.

In both cases transfers of piped drinking water are excluded.

13. Waste water treatment plants with a capacity exceeding 150 000 population equivalent as defined in Article 2 point (6) of Directive 91/271/EEC.[11]

14. Extraction of petroleum and natural gas for commercial purposes where the amount extracted exceeds 500 tonnes/day in the case of petroleum and 500 000 m^3/day in the case of gas.

15. Dams and other installations designed for the holding back or permanent storage of water, where a new or additional amount of water held back or stored exceeds 10 million cubic metres.

16. Pipelines for the transport of gas, oil or chemicals with a diameter of more than 800 mm and a length of more than 40 km.

17. Installations for the intensive rearing of poultry or pigs with more than:

    (a) 85 000 places for broilers, 60 000 places for hens;
    (b) 3000 places for production pigs (over 30 kg); or
    (c) 900 places for sows.

18. Industrial plants for the

    (a) production of pulp from timber or similar fibrous materials;
    (b) production of paper and board with a production capacity exceeding 200 tonnes per day.

19. Quarries and open-cast mining where the surface of the site exceeds 25 hectares, or peat extraction, where the surface of the site exceeds 150 hectares.

20. Construction of overhead electrical power lines with a voltage of 220 kV or more and a length of more than 15 km.

21. Installations for storage of petroleum, petrochemical, or chemical products with a capacity of 200 000 tonnes or more.

ANNEX II

Projects subject to Article 4(2)

1.   Agriculture, silviculture and aquaculture

    (a)   Projects for the restructuring of rural land holdings;

    (b)   Projects for the use of uncultivated land or semi-natural areas for intensive agricultural purposes;

    (c)   Water management projects for agriculture, including irrigation and land drainage projects;

    (d)   Initial afforestation and deforestation for the purposes of conversion to another type of land use;

    (e)   Intensive livestock installations (projects not included in Annex I);

    (f)   Intensive fish farming;

    (g)   Reclamation of land from the sea.

2.   Extractive industry

    (a)   Quarries, open-cast mining and peat extraction (projects not included in Annex I);

    (b)   Underground mining;

    (c)   Extraction of minerals by marine or fluvial dredging;

    (d)   Deep drillings, in particular:

        –   geothermal drilling,
        –   drilling for the storage of nuclear waste material,
        –   drilling for water supplies,

with the exception of drillings for investigating the stability of the soil;

(e)   Surface industrial installations for the extraction of coal, petroleum, natural gas and ores, as well as bituminous shale.

3.   Energy industry

(a)   Industrial installations for the production of electricity, steam and hot water (projects not included in Annex I);

(b)   Industrial installations for carrying gas, steam and hot water; transmission of electrical energy by overhead cables (projects not included in Annex I);

(c)   Surface storage of natural gas;

(d)   Underground storage of combustible gases;

(e)   Surface storage of fossil fuels;

(f)   Industrial briquetting of coal and lignite;

(g)   Installations for the processing and storage of radioactive waste (unless included in Annex I);

(h)   Installations for hydroelectric energy production;

(i)   Installations for the harnessing of wind power for energy production (wind farms).

4.   Production and processing of metals

(a)   Installations for the production of pig iron or steel (primary or secondary fusion) including continuous casting;

(b)   Installations for the processing of ferrous metals:

(i)   hot-rolling mills;

      (ii)   smitheries with hammers;

      (iii)   application of protective fused metal coats;

(c)   Ferrous metal foundries;

(d)   Installations for the smelting, including the alloyage, of non-ferrous metals, excluding precious metals, including recovered products (refining, foundry casting, etc.);

(e)   Installations for surface treatment of metals and plastic materials using an electrolytic or chemical process;

(f)   Manufacture and assembly of motor vehicles and manufacture of motor-vehicle engines;

(g)   Shipyards;

(h)   Installations for the construction and repair of aircraft;

(i)   Manufacture of railway equipment;

(j)   Swaging by explosives;

(k)   Installations for the roasting and sintering of metallic ores.

5.   Mineral industry

(a)   Coke ovens (dry coal distillation);

(b)   Installations for the manufacture of cement;

(c)   Installations for the production of asbestos and the manufacture of asbestos-products (projects not included in Annex I);

(d)   Installations for the manufacture of glass including glass fibre;

(e)   Installations for smelting mineral substances including the production of mineral fibres;

(f)   Manufacture of ceramic products by burning, in particular roofing tiles, bricks, refractory bricks, tiles, stoneware or porcelain.

6.   Chemical industry (projects not included in Annex I)

    (a)   Treatment of intermediate products and production of chemicals;

    (b)   Production of pesticides and pharmaceutical products, paint and varnishes, elastomers and peroxides;

    (c)   Storage facilities for petroleum, petrochemical and chemical products.

7.   Food industry

    (a)   Manufacture of vegetable and animal oils and fats;

    (b)   Packing and canning of animal and vegetable products;

    (c)   Manufacture of dairy products;

    (d)   Brewing and malting;

    (e)   Confectionery and syrup manufacture;

    (f)   Installations for the slaughter of animals;

    (g)   Industrial starch manufacturing installations;

    (h)   Fish-meal and fish-oil factories;

    (i)   Sugar factories.

8.   Textile, leather, wood and paper industries

    (a)   Industrial plants for the production of paper and board (projects not included in Annex I);

    (b)   Plants for the pretreatment (operations such as washing, bleaching, mercerization) or dyeing of fibres or textiles;

(c)   Plants for the tanning of hides and skins;

(d)   Cellulose-processing and production installations.

9.   Rubber industry

Manufacture and treatment of elastomer-based products.

10.   Infrastructure projects

(a)   Industrial estate development projects;

(b)   Urban development projects, including the construction of shopping centres and carparks

(c)   Construction of railways and intermodal transshipment facilities, and of intermodal terminals (projects not included in Annex I);

(d)   Construction of airfields (projects not included in Annex I);

(e)   Construction of roads, harbours and port installations, including fishing harbours (projects not included in Annex I);

(f)   Inland-waterway construction not included in Annex I, canalization and flood-relief works;

(g)   Dams and other installations designed to hold water or store it on a long-term basis (projects not included in Annex I);

(h)   Tramways, elevated and underground railways, suspended lines or similar lines of a particular type, used exclusively or mainly for passenger transport;

(i)   Oil and gas pipeline installations (projects not included in Annex I);

(j)   Installations of long-distance aqueducts;

(k)   Coastal work to combat erosion and maritime works capable of altering the coast through the construction, for example, of dykes, moles, jetties and other sea defence works, excluding the maintenance and reconstruction of such works;

(l)   Groundwater abstraction and artificial groundwater recharge schemes not included in Annex I;

(m)   Works for the transfer of water resources between river basins not included in Annex I.

11.   Other projects

(a)   Permanent racing and test tracks for motorized vehicles;

(b)   Installations for the disposal of waste (projects not included in Annex I);

(c)   Waste-water treatment plants (projects not included in Annex I);

(d)   Sludge-deposition sites;

(e)   Storage of scrap iron, including scrap vehicles;

(f)   Test benches for engines, turbines or reactors;

(g)   Installations for the manufacture of artificial mineral fibres;

(h)   Installations for the recovery or destruction of explosive substances;

(i)   Knackers' yards.

12.   Tourism and leisure

(a)   Ski-runs, ski-lifts and cable-cars and associated developments;

(b)   Marinas;

(c)   Holiday villages and hotel complexes outside urban areas and associated developments;

(d)   Permanent camp sites and caravan sites;

(e)   Theme parks.

13.   –   Any change or extension of projects listed in Annex I or Annex II, already authorized, executed or in the process of being executed, which may have significant adverse effects on the environment;

       –   Projects in Annex I, undertaken exclusively or mainly for the development and testing of new methods or products and not used for more than two years.

ANNEX III

Selection criteria referred to in Article 4(3)

1.   Characteristics of projects

The characteristics of projects must be considered having regard, in particular, to:

   –   the size of the project,
   –   the cumulation with other projects,
   –   the use of natural resources,
   –   the production of waste,
   –   pollution and nuisances,
   –   the risk of accidents, having regard in particular to substances or technologies used.

2.   Location of projects

The environmental sensitivity of geographical areas likely to be affected by projects must be considered, having regard, in particular, to:

   –   the existing land use,
   –   the relative abundance, quality and regenerative capacity of natural resources in the area,
   –   the absorption capacity of the natural environment, paying particular attention to the

following areas:

(a)   wetlands;

(b)   coastal zones;

(c)   mountain and forest areas;

(d)   nature reserves and parks;

(e)   areas classified or protected under Member States' legislation; special protection areas designated by Member States pursuant to Directive 79/409/EEC and 92/43/EEC;

(f)   areas in which the environmental quality standards laid down in Community legislation have already been exceeded;

(g)   densely populated areas;

(h)   landscapes of historical, cultural or archaeological significance.

3.   Characteristics of the potential impact

The potential significant effects of projects must be considered in relation to criteria set out under 1 and 2 above, and having regard in particular to:

–   the extent of the impact (geographical area and size of the affected population),

–   the transfrontier nature of the impact,

–   the magnitude and complexity of the impact,

–   the probability of the impact,

–   the duration, frequency and reversibility of the impact.

ANNEX IV

Information referred to in Article 5(1)

1.   Description of the project, including in particular:

–   a description of the physical characteristics of the whole project and the land-use requirements during the construction and operational phases,

–   a description of the main characteristics of the production processes, for instance, nature and quantity of the materials used,

       –   an estimate, by type and quantity, of expected residues and emissions (water, air and soil pollution, noise, vibration, light, heat, radiation, etc.) resulting from the operation of the proposed project.

2.   An outline of the main alternatives studied by the developer and an indication of the main reasons for this choice, taking into account the environmental effects.

3.   A description of the aspects of the environment likely to be significantly affected by the proposed project, including, in particular, population, fauna, flora, soil, water, air, climatic factors, material assets, including the architectural and archaeological heritage, landscape and the interrelationship between the above factors.

4.   A description[12] of the likely significant effects of the proposed project on the environment resulting from:

       –   the existence of the project,
       –   the use of natural resources,
       –   the emission of pollutants, the creation of nuisances and the elimination of waste,
       –   and the description by the developer of the forecasting methods used to assess the effects on the environment.

5.   A description of the measures envisaged to prevent, reduce and where possible offset any significant adverse effects on the environment.

6.   A non-technical summary of the information provided under the above headings.

     An indication of any difficulties (technical deficiencies or lack of know-how) encountered by the developer in compiling the required information.

Notes

1.   *OJ*, C130, 12 May 1994, p. 8.
2.   *OJ*, C393, 31 December 1994, p. 1.

3.   *OJ*, C210, 14 August 1995, p. 78.

4.   European Parliament Opinion of 11 October 1995 (*OJ*, C287, 30 October 1995, p. 101), Council Common Position of 25 June 1996 (*OJ*, C248, 26 August 1996, p. 75) and European Parliament Decision of 13 November 1996 (*OJ*, C362, 2 December 1996, p. 103).

5.   *OJ*, L175, 5 July 1985, p. 40. Directive as last amended by the 1994 Act of Accession.

6.   *OJ*, L103, 25 April 1979, p. 1. Directive as last amended by the 1994 Act of Accession.

7.   *OJ*, L206, 22 July 1992, p. 7.

8.   *OJ*, L257, 10 October 1996, p. 26.

9.   *OJ*, L194, 25 September 1975, p. 39. Directive as last amended by Commission Decision 94/3/EC (*OJ*, L5, 7 January 1994, p. 15).

10.   *OJ*, L377, 31 December 1991, p. 20. Directive as last amended by Directive 94/31/EC (*OJ*, L168, 2 July 1994, p. 28).

11.   *OJ*, L135, 30 May 1991, p. 40. Directive as last amended by the 1994 Act of Accession.

12.   This description should cover the direct and and indirect, secondary, cumulative, short-, medium- and long-term, permanent and temporary, positive and negative effects of the project.

Suggested Answers to Examples

Suggested answer – example 1

The number of possible answers to this question are almost limitless so don't expect to have a solution which looks like this! The purpose of this exercise has been to illustrate the kind of problems encountered in scoping and it should be noted that the background of whoever tries this exercise will have a profound effect on how the priorities for the impacts are perceived. For example, an ecologist would be expected to be most concerned with the potential impacts to the invertebrates. Note also that more than one piece of baseline information would be required in order to predict each potential impact properly.

	Impact	*Baseline information*
1.	Visual	Landscape characteristics
2.	Traffic congestion	Current traffic levels
3.	Loss of dragonfly species	Dragonfly survey
4.	Disease	Number of pests
5.	Odour	Prevailing wind data
6.	Stream water quality	Biological oxygen demand
7.	Housing devaluation	Existing property prices
8.	Windblown litter increase	Proportion of waste which is paper
9.	Loss of agricultural land	Affected agricultural land classification

Suggested answer – example 2

The two extracts are both taken from real environmental impact statements, although they are now read out of context for the purposes of this exercise.

The first extract is the better of the two as it quantifies the impact and places it in context with regard to the national picture. It states, quite clearly, that destruction of hedgerow will occur, and that it is hedgerow of moderate interest with respect to species richness.

The second extract, by contrast, contains no quantified information and is exceptionally vague. We are left in considerable doubt as to what a 'material number of birds or mammals' represents, or even what the species involved are – could they be rare? It is not adequate to state that there will be 'no impact' in areas adjacent to the site without explaining why. Phrasing such as this makes the reader suspicious rather than allaying any fears about the fate of fauna as a result of the development.

Suggested answer – example 3

1.   A typical wind turbine generator is 30 m high with a further 30 m diameter of rotating blades. As a result it is difficult to hide. Currently, standard practice is to look at blade design – it is concluded from the results of surveys that three blades are more acceptable than two – and also at the colour of the wind turbines, a neutral colour like grey making them blend into the environment much more. Apart from these measures, which would do little to appease residents living very close to a windfarm, the only other feasible measures are to plant woodland close to the affected houses to restrict their view, and to site the turbines as sympathetically as possible given that they work most efficiently on hill tops!

2.   Several options exist for such impacts:

  •   The easiest and most effective would be to install double-glazing at the dwelling. This solution is far from ideal as it then relies on the windows remaining closed.
  •   Another solution would be some form of noise barrier between the dwelling and the quarry. Woodland can form this function reasonably well, but there is a finite time, as it grows, before an effective barrier results.

- Realistically, the mitigation measure which is found to be acceptable for this kind of problem is that of good working practice, whereby blasting times are limited to certain hours which have the least possible effects on nearby residents. It should again be stressed that EIA is not a method of stopping development, and in this case would serve to reduce this particular impact without jeopardising the feasibility of the development.

3.   The simplest and most common solution to this problem would be to raise the height of the discharge stack of the power station so that the pollution disperses into the atmosphere more and affects a wider area of environment at far more diffuse levels. This is the kind of action that ultimately leads to the destruction of forests due to acid rain in a downwind direction and it creates a greater visual impact. A more ideal solution, though a more expensive one, would be to use scrubbers in the stack to remove the pollution at source.

4.   This problem arises as a result of the increase in traffic, and care must be taken over the mitigation measures: a diversion of the traffic can help one location, but causes problems elsewhere. The sensitivity of various locations needs to be assessed. The difficulty inherent in dealing with problems such as these is what leads to policy decisions so that, for example, catalytic converters become standard equipment for vehicles.

5.   This example was included to demonstrate that project EIA has its limitations and effective consideration of some environmental problems requires EIA of policies. This example, it could be argued, could be mitigated by increasing the use of public transport at the expense of private vehicles. This is beyond the scope of project EIA.

Bibliography

The aim of this bibliography is to:

- present a list of books which, in the author's opinion, are important in the field with relevance to EIA in the UK either directly or because of their presentation of best practice – no attempt has been made to provide an exhaustive list of EIA texts which would be of value to academics only;

- present a list of journals which, in the author's opinion, are useful journals for those with an interest in EIA in the UK – again, their value has been assessed considering both direct relevance to the UK and their consideration of best practice;

- present a list of the official guidance published by the relevant government departments over the years to explain the EIA procedures in the UK;

- present a list of website addresses (URLs) which provide useful and up-to-date information on EIA matters of relevance to the UK or which contain useful information on best practice – only pages maintained by established organisations have been included as their existence on the web is likely to be more than ephemeral in nature;

- present a list of references cited in writing this book.

Books

Barrow, C.J. (1997) *Environmental and Social Impact Assessment: An Introduction*. Arnold. 310 pp. ISBN: 0 340 66271 9.

Biswas, A.K. and Agarwala, S.B.C. (1992) *Environmental Impact Assessment for Developing Countries.* Butterworth Heinemann. 249 pp. ISBN: 0-7506-2139-7.

British Medical Association (1998) *Health and Environmental Impact Assessment.* Earthscan. 243 pp. ISBN: 1 85383 541-2.

Canter, L.W. (1996) *Environmental Impact Assessment,* 2nd edn. McGraw-Hill. 660 pp. ISBN: 0-07-114103-0.

Department of the Environment (1989) *Environmental Assessment: A Guide to the Procedures.* HMSO 64 pp. ISBN: 0-11-752244-9.

Donnelly, A., Dalal-Clayton, B. and Hughes, R. (1998) *A Directory of Impact Assessment Guidelines,* 2nd edn. International Institute for Environment and Development, London. 211 pp. ISBN: 1 899825 11 8.

Environmental Law Network International (eds) (1997) *International Environmental Impact Assessment. European and Comparative Law and Practical Experience. Contributions of the International Conference held in Milan in October 1996.* Cameron May, London. 276 pp. ISBN: 1 874698 07 4.

Gilpin, A. (1995) *Environmental Impact Assessment (EIA): Cutting Edge for the Twenty-first Century.* Cambridge University Press. 182 pp. ISBN: 0-521-42967-6.

Glasson, J., Therivel, R. and Chadwick, A. (1999) *Introduction to Environmental Impact Assessment. Principles and Procedures, Process, Practice and Prospects,* 2nd edn. UCL Press. 496 pp. ISBN: 1-85728-945-5.

Harrop, D.O. and Nixon, J.A. (1999) *Environmental Assessment in Practice.* Routledge, London. 219 pp. ISBN: 0-415-15691-2.

Institute of Environmental Assessment (1995) *Guidelines for Baseline Ecological Assessment.* E&FN Spon, London. 142 pp. ISBN: 0-419-20510-1.

Landscape Institute and Institute of Environmental Assessment (1995) *Guidelines for Landscape and Visual Impact Assessment.* E&FN Spon, London. 126 pp. ISBN: 0-419-20380-X.

Moore, V. (1992) *A Practical Approach to Planning Law*, 3rd edn. Blackstone Press. 381 pp. ISBN: 1-85431-239-1.

Morris, P. and Therivel, R. (1995) *Methods of Environmental Impact Assessment.* UCL Press. 378 pp. ISBN: 1-85728-215-9.

O'Sullivan, P., McKirdy, B., Askarieh, M., Bond, A., Russell, S., Dagg, S., Russell, I., Alonso, J. and Santiago, J.L. (1999) *Environmental Impact Assessments and Geological Repositories for Radioactive Waste. Final Report: Volume 1 – Main Report.* Report to the European Commission (DG XI), EC Contracts B4-3070/97/000821/MAR/C3 and B4-3040/98/000429/MAR/C3. 100 pp.

Petts, J. (ed.) (1999a) *Handbook of Environmental Impact Assessment. Volume 1. Environmental Impact Assessment: Process, Methods and Potential.* Blackwell Science. 484 pp. ISBN: 0-632-04772-0.

Petts, J. (ed.) (1999b) *Handbook of Environmental Impact Assessment. Volume 2. Environmental Impact Assessment in Practice: Impact and Limitations.* Blackwell Science. 450 pp. ISBN: 0-632-04771-2.

Sadar, M.H. (1996) *Environmental Impact Assessment*, 2nd edn. Francophone Secretariat of the International Association for Impact Assessment, Montreal, Canada. 191 pp. ISBN: 2 922600 00 9.

Scott, J. (1998) *EC Environmental Law.* Longman. 189 pp. ISBN: 0-582-29190-9.

Sheate, W. (1996) *Environmental Impact Assessment: Law and Policy. Making an Impact II.* Cameron May, London. 300 pp. ISBN: 1 874698 910.

Therivel, R. and Partidário, M.R. (1996) *The Practice of Strategic Environmental Assessment.* Earthscan. 206 pp. ISBN: 1-85383-373-8.

Therivel, R., Wilson, E., Thompson, S., Heaney, D. and Pritchard, D. (1992) *Strategic Environmental Assessment.* Earthscan. 181 pp. ISBN: 1-85383-147-6.

Vanclay, F. and Bronstein, D.A. (1995) *Environmental and Social Impact Assessment.* John Wiley & Sons. 325 pp. ISBN: 0-471-95764-X.

Wathern, P. (1998) *Environmental Impact Assessment: Theory and Practice*. Routledge. 332 pp. ISBN: 0-415-07884-9.

Wood, C. (1995) *Environmental Impact Assessment: A Comparative Review*. Longman Scientific & Technical. 337 pp. ISBN: 0-582-23696-7.

Journals and magazines

ENDS Report. ISSN: 0966-4076.

Environment and Planning A. ISSN: 0308-518X.

Environmental Assessment (magazine of the Institute of Environmental Assessment). ISSN: 1351-0738.

Environmental Impact Assessment Review. ISSN: 0195-9255.

Environmental Monitoring and Assessment. ISSN: 0167-6369.

Impact Assessment and Project Appraisal. ISSN: 1461-5517.

Journal of Environmental Assessment Policy and Management. ISSN: 1464-3332.

Journal of Environmental Management. ISSN: 0301-4797.

Journal of Environmental Planning and Management. ISSN: 0964-0568.

Local Environment. ISSN: 1354-9839.

Town Planning Review. ISSN: 0041-0020.

Urban Studies. ISSN: 0042-0980.

Official guidance

Taken from DETR web page: http://www.planning.detr.gov.uk/eia/assess/doc12.htm.

Planning – England and Wales

Department of the Environment (1988) *Environmental Assessment.* Circular 15/88 (Welsh Office 23/88). Stationery Office, London.

Department of the Environment (1992) *Publicity for Planning Applications.* Circular 15/92 (Welsh Office 32/92) (paras 15–16 refer to EA). Stationery Office, London.

Department of the Environment (1992) *The Town and Country Planning General Regulations 1992/The Town and Country Planning (Development Plans and Consultation) Directions 1992.* Circular 19/92 (Welsh Office 39/92) (paras 36–40 refer to EA). Stationery Office, London.

Department of the Environment (1994) *Environmental Assessment: Amendment of Regulations.* Circular 7/94 (Welsh Office 20/94). Stationery Office, London.

Department of the Environment (1995) *Permitted Development and Environmental Assessment.* Circular 3/95 (Welsh Office 12/95). Stationery Office, London.

Department of the Environment (1995) *The Use of Conditions in Planning Permissions.* Circular 11/95 (para. 77 refers to EA). Stationery Office, London.

Department of the Environment (1995) *The Town and Country Planning (Environmental Assessment and Unauthorised Development) Regulations 1995.* Circular 13/95 (Welsh Office 39/95). Stationery Office, London.

Planning – Scotland

Scottish Development Department (1988) *Environmental Assessment: Implementation of EC Directive: The Environmental Assessment (Scotland) Regulations 1988.* Circular 13/88. Stationery Office, London.

Scottish Development Department (1988) *Environmental Assessment of Projects in Simplified Planning Zones and Enterprise Zones.* Circular 26/88. Stationery Office, London.

Scottish Office Environment Department (1994) *The Environmental Assessment (Scotland) Amendment Regulations 1994.* Circular 26/94. Stationery Office, London.

Scottish Development Department (1997) *Environmental Assessment and (i) Planning Enforcement Appeals; and (ii) Permitted Development.* Circular 25/1997. Stationery Office, London.

Planning – Northern Ireland

Department of the Environment (Northern Ireland) (1989) *Environmental Impact Assessment.* Development Control Advice Note No. 10. Stationery Office, London.

Guidance relating to environmental assessment outside the planning system

Crown Estate Office (1988) *Environmental Assessment of Marine Salmon Farms.* Stationery Office, London.

Department of Trade and Industry (1992) *Guidance on Environmental Assessment of Cross-Country Pipelines.* Stationery Office, London.

Department of Transport (1992) *Transport and Works Act 1992: a guide to procedures for obtaining orders relating to transport systems, inland waterways and works interfering with rights of navigation.* Stationery Office, London.

Department of Transport/Scottish Office Industry Department/The Welsh Office/Department of the Environment for Northern Ireland (1993) *Environmental Assessment: the Design Manual for Roads and Bridges.* Stationery Office, London.

Overseas Development Administration (1992) *Manual of Environmental Appraisal.* Stationery Office, London.

Forestry Commission (1993) *Environmental Assessment of New Woodlands.* Stationery Office, London.

General guidance

Department of the Environment/Welsh Office (1989) *Environmental Assessment: A Guide to the Procedures*. Stationery Office, London.

Department of the Environment (1995) *Preparation of Environmental Statements for Planning Projects that Require Environmental Assessment: A Good Practice Guide*. Research Report. Stationery Office, London.

Copies of the above guidance may be purchased from the Stationery Office. In addition, the following *free* publications may be available

Department of the Environment (1997) *Environmental Assessment*. Department of the Environment.

Department of the Environment and Welsh Office (1995) *Your Permitted Development Rights and Environmental Assessment*. Department of the Environment.

Welsh Office (n.d.) *Environmental Assessment/Assu'r Amgylchedd*. Welsh Office.

Scottish Office (n.d.) *Environmental Assessment – a Guide*. Scottish Office.

Research reports

Bellanger, C. and Frost, F. (1997) *Directory of Environmental Impact Statements July 1988 – January 1997*. Working Paper No. 171. Impacts Assessment Unit, Oxford Brookes University. 234 pp. (Note that this working paper is regularly updated – contact the Impacts Assessment Unit for the most recent version on 01865 483448.)

EIA Centre, University of Manchester (1991) *Monitoring Environmental Assessment and Planning*. Stationery Office, London. ISBN. 0-11-752436-0.

Environmental Resources Management (1997) *Mitigation Measures in Environmental Statements*. DETR Publications. ISBN: 1-85112-050-5.

Land Use Consultants (1994) *Good Practice on the Evaluation of Environmental Information for Planning Projects*. Stationery Office, London. ISBN: 0-11-752990-7.

Land Use Consultants (1994) *Evaluation of Environmental Information for Planning Projects: A Good Practice Guide*. Stationery Office, London. ISBN: 0-11-753043-3.

Oxford Brookes University (1996) *Changes in the Quality of Environmental Statements for Planning Projects – Research Report*. Stationery Office, London. ISBN: 0-11-753269-X.

Web pages

Australian EIA Network: http://www.erin.gov.au/portfolio/epg/eianet/eianet.html

Canadian Environmental Assessment Agency: http://www.ceaa.gc.ca/

Department of Environment, Transport and the Regions Environmental Assessment page:

http://www.planning.detr.gov.uk/eia/assess/index.htm

EIA Centre of Manchester University: http://www.art.man.ac.uk/eia/EIAC.HTM

EIA Unit of the European Commission: http://europa.eu.int/comm/dg11/eia/home.htm

Institute of Environmental Management and Assessment, Lincoln and Edinburgh, UK: http://www.iema.net/

International Association for Impact Assessment (based in the USA): http://www.iaia.org/

Oxford Brookes University's Impacts Assessment Unit: http://www.brookes.ac.uk/schools/planning/research/iau/iau.html

Penelope Project, Imperial College, London (has information on UK EIA legislation and case studies): http://www-penelope.th.ic.ac.uk/

United States Council on Environmental Quality (CEQ) regulations can be found at: http://ceq.eh.doe.gov/nepa/regs/ceq/toc_ceq.htm

US CEQ scoping guidance can be found at: http://ceq.eh.doe.gov/nepa/regs/scope/scoping.htm

University of Wales Aberystwyth's EIA Unit: http://www.aber.ac.uk/environment

References

Andrews, R.N.L. (1976) *Environmental Policy and Administrative Change*. Lexington Books, 230 pp.

Anon. (1989) *European Community Law: An Overview*. HLT Publications, London. 83 pp.

Anon. (1992) 'The mineral planning survey of IDO registration', *Mineral Planning*, **52**, 21–2.

Anon. (1996) 'Questions of *locus standi*', *Environmental Law Monthly*, July 1996, 10–12.

Anon. (1999) 'House of Lords judgment forces EIA on old minerals permissions', *ENDS Report*, **293**, p.39.

Arnstein, S.R. (1969) 'A ladder of citizen participation', *Journal of the American Institute of Planners*, **35(4)**, 216–44.

Bardach, E. and Pugliaresi, L. (1977) 'The environmental impact statement vs. the real world', *Public Interest*, February, 22–8.

Barker, A. and Wood, C. (1999) 'An evaluation of EIA system performances in eight EU countries', *Environmental Impact Assessment Review*, **19(4)**, 387–404.

Barrow, C.J. (1997) *Environmental and Social Impact Assessment: An Introduction*. Arnold. 310 pp.

Beanlands, G. (1988) 'Scoping methods and baseline studies in EIA', in Wathern, P. (ed.), *Environmental Impact Assessment: Theory and Practice*. Routledge, pp. 33–46.

Bisset, R. (1991) *Monitoring and Auditing of Impacts: A Review*. CEMP 6th intensive course on environmental assessment and management, 30 June to 20 September 1991. 32 pp.

Bond, A.J. (1997) 'Environmental assessment and planning: a chronology of development in England and Wales', *Journal of Environmental Planning and Management*, **40(2)**, 261–71.

Briffett, C. (1999) 'Environmental impact assessment in East Asia', in Petts, J. (ed.), *Handbook of Environmental Impact Assessment. Volume 2. Environmental Impact Assessment in Practice: Impact and Limitations*. Blackwell Science, pp. 143–67.

Brito, E. and Verocai, I. (1999) 'Environmental impact assessment in South and Central America', in Petts, J. (ed.), *Handbook of Environmental Impact Assessment. Volume 2. Environmental Impact Assessment in Practice: Impact and Limitations*. Blackwell Science, pp. 183–202.

Brooks, S. (1991) *The environmental assessment of wind energy projects in five European countries: Belgium, Denmark, Germany, Netherlands, and the United Kingdom*. MSc Thesis, University of Wales Aberystwyth.

Canter, L. (1984) 'Environmental impact studies in the United States', in Clark, B.D., Bisset, R., Gilad, A. and Tomlinson, P. (eds), *Perspectives on Environmental Impact Assessment*. D. Reidel, pp. 15–24.

Canter, L.W. (1996) *Environmental Impact Assessment*, 2nd edn. McGraw-Hill, 660 pp.

Carson, R. (1963) *Silent Spring*. Hamish Hamilton, 304 pp.

Commission of the European Communities (1980) *Council Directive relating to the quality of water intended for human consumption*. L229, Office for Official Publications of the European Communities, Luxembourg.

Commission of the European Communities (1993) *Report from the Commission of the Implementation of Directive 85/337/EEC on the Assessment of the Effects of Certain Public and Private Projects on the Environment*, COM (93) 28 final, volumes 1–13. Office for Official Publications of the European Communities, Luxembourg.

Commission of the European Communities (1994a) *Environmental Impact Assessment Review Checklist*. European Commission, DG XI, Brussels, Belgium. 29 pp.

Commission of the European Communities (1994b) *Proposal for a Council Directive amending Directive 85/337/EEC on the assessment of the effects of certain public and private projects on the environment*, COM (93) 575 final. Office for Official Publications of the European Communities, Luxembourg. 25 pp.

Commission of the European Communities (1997) *Update of the five-year review.* European Commission, DG XI, Brussels, Belgium. 103 pp. Also available from: http://europa.eu.int/comm/dg11/eia/eia-support.htm [Accessed 11/11/99].

Council on Environmental Quality (1978) 'National Environmental Policy Act – Regulations', *Federal Register*, **43**, 55978–6007.

CPRE (1992) *Environmental Assessment and Planning: Extension of Application.* CPRE's response to the government's consultation paper. CPRE, London. 13 pp.

Culhane, P.J. (1993) 'Post-EIS environmental auditing: a first step to making rational environmental assessment a reality', *Environmental Professional*, **15**, 66–75.

Department of the Environment/Welsh Office (1989) *Environmental Assessment: A Guide to the Procedures.* HMSO. 64 pp.

DETR (1995) *Preparation of Environmental Statements for Planning Projects that Require Environmental Assessment: A Good Practice Guide.* HMSO. 134 pp.

DETR (1997a) *Consultation Paper: Implementation of EC Directive (97/11/EC) on Environmental Assessment.* DETR, London, 28 July 1997. 39 pp.

DETR (1997b) *Consultation Paper: Determining the need for Environmental Assessment (EC Directive 97/11/EC).* DETR, London, 19 December 1997. 30 pp.

DETR (1998) *Draft Town and Country Planning (Assessment of Environmental Effects) Regulations 1998.* DETR, London, 16 July 1998. 55 pp.

DETR (1999) *Environmental Impact Assessment.* DETR Circular 02/99. Stationery Office, London. 43 pp.

Dipper, B., Jones, C. and Wood, C. (1998) 'Monitoring and post-auditing in environmental impact assessment: a review', *Journal of Environmental Planning and Management*, **41(6)**, 731–47.

Donnelly, A., Dalal-Clayton, B. and Hughes, R. (1998) *A Directory of Impact Assessment Guidelines*, 2nd edn. International Institute for Environment and Development, London. 211 pp.

Economic Commission for Europe (1990) *Environmental Series 3: Post-Project Analysis in Environmental Impact Assessment.* United Nations, New York. 54 pp.

European Council (1985) 'Directive on the assessment of the effects of certain public and private projects on the environment, 85/337/EEC', *Official Journal of the European Communities,* **L175,** 40–8.

European Council (1997) 'Directive 97/11/EC of 3 March amending Directive 85/337/EEC on the assessment of the effects of certain public and private projects on the environment', *Official Journal of the European Communities,* **L73,** 14 March 1997.

European Economic Community (1967) *Treaty setting up The European Economic Community, Rome, 25th March, 1957.* HMSO, London. 231 pp.

Federal Environmental Assessment Review Office (1978) *Guide for Environmental Screening.* Ottawa, Federal Environmental Assessment Review Office.

Federal Environmental Assessment Review Office (1988) *Manual on Public Involvement in Environmental Assessment: Planning and Implementing Public Involvement Programs.* Volume 2. Ottawa, Federal Environmental Assessment Review Office. p. 9.

Gilpin, A. (1995) *Environmental Impact Assessment (EIA): Cutting Edge for the Twenty-first Century.* Cambridge University Press. 182 pp.

Glasson, J., Therivel, R. and Chadwick, A. (1994) *Introduction to Environmental Impact Assessment. Principles and Procedures, Process, Practice and Prospects.* UCL Press. 342 pp.

Hall, P. (1992) *Urban and Regional Planning,* 3rd edn. Routledge, pp. 12–30.

Hildén, M., Valve, H., Jónsdóttir, S., Balfors, B., Faith-Ell, C., Moen, B., Peuhkuri, T., Schmidtbauer, J., Swensen, I. and Tesli, A. (1998) *EIA and Its Application for Policies, Plans and Programmes in Sweden, Finland, Iceland and Norway.* TemaNord Environment, Nordic Council of Ministers, Copenhagen. 169 pp.

Jones, C.E. (1995) 'The effect of environmental assessment on planning decisions', *Reports for the Natural and Built Environment Professions,* **9,** 5–7.

Kakonge, J.O. (1999) 'Environmental impact assessment in Africa', in Petts, J. (ed.), *Handbook of Environmental Impact Assessment. Volume 2. Environmental Impact Assessment in Practice: Impact and Limitations*. Blackwell Science, pp. 168–82.

Kramer, L. (1992) *Focus on European Environmental Law*. Sweet & Maxwell, 321 pp.

Lee, N. and Colley, R. (1992) *Reviewing the Quality of Environmental Statements*. Occasional Paper No. 24, 2nd edn. EIA Centre, University of Manchester, 52 pp.

Lee, N., Colley, R., Bonde, J. and Simpson, J. (1999) *Reviewing the Quality of Environmental Statements and Environmental Appraisals*. Occasional Paper No. 55. EIA Centre, University of Manchester, 52 pp.

Macrory, R. (1994) 'First European Court ruling on environmental assessment', *ENDS Report*, **237**, 43.

Macrory, R. (1997) 'European Court extends scope of environmental assessment rules', *ENDS Report*, **264**, 44–5.

Macrory, R. (1998) 'Environmental assessment and the duty to give reasons', *ENDS Report*, **283**, 47.

Macrory, R. (1999a) 'Environmental assessment legally required for road schemes', *ENDS Report*, **292**, 53.

Macrory, R. (1999b) 'European Court continues to extend reach of EIA Directive', *ENDS Report*, **297**, 58–9.

O'Sullivan, P. and Bond, A.J. (1999) *Environmental Impacts Assessments and Geological Repositories for Radioactive Waste. EC Contracts B4-3070/97/000821/MAR/C3 and B4-3040/98/000429/MAR/C3. Volume 4: Workshop Report.* Nirex UK Ltd, EIA Unit, ENRESA, ONDRAF/NIRAS and SKB.

Petts, J. (1999) 'Public participation and environmental impact assessment', in Petts, J. (ed.) *Handbook of Environmental Impact Assessment. Volume 1. Environmental Impact Assessment: Process, Methods and Potential.* Blackwell Science, pp. 145–77.

Ramsay, C.G. (1984) 'Assessment of hazard and risk', in Clark, B.D., Bisset, R., Gilad, A. and Tomlinson, P. (eds), *Perspectives on Environmental Impact Assessment*. D. Reidel, pp. 133–60.

Rzeszot, U.A. (1999) 'Environmental impact assessment in Central and Eastern Europe', in Petts, J. (ed.), *Handbook of Environmental Impact Assessment. Volume 2. Environmental Impact Assessment in Practice: Impact and Limitations*. Blackwell Science, pp. 121–42.

Scott, J. (1998) *EC Environmental Law*. Longman (European Law Series). 189 pp.

Sheate, W. (1996) *Environmental Impact Assessment: Law and Policy. Making an Impact II*. Cameron May, 300 pp.

Sippe, R. (1999) 'Criteria and standards for assessing significant impacts', in Petts, J. (ed.), *Handbook of Environmental Impact Assessment. Volume 1. Environmental Impact Assessment: Process, Methods and Potential*. Blackwell Science, pp. 74–92.

Smith, D.B. and van der Wansen, M. (1995) *Strengthening EIA Capacity in Asia: Environmental Impact Assessment in the Philippines, Indonesia, and Sri Lanka*. World Resources Institute, Washington DC. 90 pp.

Smythe, R.B. (1997) 'The historical roots of NEPA', in Clark, R. and Canter, L. (eds), *Environmental Policy and NEPA: Past, Present and Future*. St Lucie Press, Florida, pp. 3–14.

United Nations Economic Commission for Europe (UNECE) (1991) *Convention on Environmental Impact Assessment in a Transboundary Context*. United Nations, Geneva. 22 pp. Also available from: http://www.unece.org/env/eia/eia.htm [Accessed 11/10/99].

United Nations Economic Commission for Europe (UNECE) (1999) *Signatory List for the Århus Convention* [online]. Available from: http://www.unece.org/env/europe/signat.htm [Accessed 15/07/99].

Walker, L.J. and Johnston, J. (1999) *Guidelines for the Assessment of Indirect and Cumulative Impacts as well as Impact Interactions*. EC DG XI, Brussels. 126 pp.

Wathern, P. (1988) *Environmental Impact Assessment: Theory and Practice*. Routledge, 332 pp.

Wolf, C.P. (1983) 'The U.S. model of environmental impact assessment', in PADC (eds), *Environmental Impact Assessment*. Martinus Nijhoff, pp. 21–40.

Wood, C. (1995) *Environmental Impact Assessment: A Comparative Review*. Longman Scientific & Technical. 337 pp.

Wood, C. (1999) 'Comparative evaluation of environmental impact assessment systems', in Petts, J. (ed.), *Handbook of Environmental Impact Assessment. Volume 2. Environmental Impact Assessment in Practice: Impact and Limitations*. Blackwell Science, pp. 10–34.

Index